Cherries

by xxx

This book is a work of fiction. Names, characters, places, and incidents either are products of the author's imagination or are used fictitiously. Any resemblance to actual persons, living or dead, events, or locales is entirely coincidental.

All rights reserved. No part of this book may be reproduced or transmitted in any form or by any means, electronic or mechanical, including photocopying, recording, or by any information storage and retrieval system without the written permission of the author, except where permitted by law.

To contact the author email   cherriesbyxxx@gmail.com

cherries by xxx i to r index

I can sit down

I cant overestimate

I dont feel continue

I dont feel

I dont know once again

I dont wanna

I feel like I m cheating

I guess so

I just cant

I m glad

I m not dying

I m sorry but

I m sorry

I think i

I think on some

I ve come a long way

Internet without the hassle

Is gonna die

It is now

It s time to stop

It's a gun it s a gun it s a gun

Jeff

Kai ti ekana

Limited access

Lunchbreak

Mai laptop

Many people

Me and john

Mistreating me

Mm are you happy

Mmm so frustrating

Mmm yoga

My book publishers

My fuckin neighbours

New everything

New Text Document

Nice tip

No but

No I mean

No real what

Noo o

Nothing ever prepares me

O k so

Ok ime

Ok so so

Ok so the film

Ok so what have we got

Ok so

Ok still

Orgasm

Parapente text

Pes mu

Plan be

Pple I said no to

Psychanalisis

Read

Right then

cherries by xxx

i to r

this first section contains only the first page of each story

got it?

During times of universal deceit telling the truth becomes a revolutionary act
George orwell

During times of universal deceit telling the truth becomes a revolutionary act
George orwell

During times of universal deceit telling the truth becomes a revolutionary act
George orwell

During times of universal deceit telling the truth becomes a revolutionary act
George orwell

During times of universal deceit telling the truth becomes a revolutionary act
George orwell

During times of universal deceit telling the truth becomes a revolutionary act
George orwell

During times of universal deceit telling the truth becomes a revolutionary act
George orwell

Right then

Every day is a new day

And you have to treat it like that

Not like a continuation of the old day

An old day

Any old day

And time to reflect is a bit like a waste of time

Or not

I mean today I woke up with my boyf we went out to the park he was feeling a bit shit

And so was I to one level

I had have to endure the flatmate once again

It was a difficult morning

I mean the girl wont shut up talkin shit out of her ass

I mean really

Now maybe she apologises

I think she should

I mean really

What was that about

He is only nice to you

She finds me in times when I m happy and tired

Anyway I mean

Then we played chess

It wasn't relaxing

I m sorry

I can t relax over there at the moment

I ll have to talk to her

Yes I will

I can sit down

I can sit down and have a little swim in my own poo

That's what I feel like

That s my next project

Reflections on the fourth of may 2013- no it s june

In may it was very different

In june it s like ha- im fuckin lovin it!

You know this artist that they made her paint the imprints on the wall because

Just because really

With no explanation

And you know no fuss she did it

Little did they know they were going to regret it so fast

I just got interrupted by my friend simon

Another big ego

So it s about big egos really isn't it

If I have one I hide it really well

I think that s why I like swimming in my own pool

So I mean really I mean I m enjoying the attention but to be honest

I mean really

What do u know

Little do they know about things

About life

No I don't want to be nasty and horrible

The power of words

The power of cold

The power of knowledge

The power of so cold knowledge

The power of you and me

On the sofa

The power so far

The power so far ahead

The power so far ahead up your ass

The power of an umbrella

The power of you and me

The power the power the power of not being dyslexic

The power of running ahead knowingly

Not knowingly

The power of not knowingly

The power of you and me

The power of who u like

To be

M

The power of you and me

M

The power of mixtrust and new emotions

The new me

The new you and me

The power of light

The light

The power of dreams

Ok so am I really showing this piece

I mean am i

I mean I should

I mean it s a thought

A scary thought

Somehow harmless if you consider the physical body to be one that dies anyway

In the grand scheme of things it s not a massive gesture anyway

Would you say it would be classed as a jealous type of crime

But why

We allocate things ruthlessly allover the place

I m looking for the word

Senselessly, authaireta/ mmm I ll look it up

What do you know

What do u know

My friend simon is the only guy I know that actually tried to kill someone

By giving him lots of heroin

I felt priviledged he told me the story and I could totally see where he s coming from

My friend simon is someone I respect and love and I would forgive anything anyway

Socrates had said that "geniouses should be allowed to blabla and scandalise their uncles"2

Socrates was a pretty cool guy I presume with lots of time on his hands for spiritual cultivating1

Bit like gardening

Today,m he would live in essex in a villa, his son would be a plumber and he himself would have grown out of the roofer s business, with a profound mindfulness acquired from doing

As opposed to non doing

Yoga says: if you feel down, shit, frustrated, throw yourself into selfless service,,,

mmm. interesting, yoga to me is like an uncle that knows what he s talking about

but I may still choose to do the wrong thing

ah and there is no right or wrong anyway

Comfortable with that coment

;; it s not fair – you got a girlfriend it s not fair;;

I would feel less comfortable if you swallowed your tongue

Bit more comfortable if the bone of your nose went into your brain

Is it too much to ask

Why

Why do we classify crimes so unfairly

I d like to see the end of your nose sticking out through the back of your head

Now I feel better, good, now I can say I can let that one go

But not now

As this hasn't happened yet

I m telling you – people die

All the time

It s not fair

Why is it not fair

I think it s not fair I m not allowed to stick the fork in your eye

And I think I m right

And you know justice is a big joke an entrepreneur s business anyway

Oh sweet

This is the material for my Halloween nite

Hallo ☺

What just happened

I set my own boundaries

I explained my point of view

I gave options

And it backfired

What about what about

What about how I feel

Once again

Ok mum

Hi mum

Mum?

#you have got to be an idiot

And I get it

It s just I don't want to be with an idiot

You cant be an idiot if you re with me

And in the end of the day it s all come clear

You can t be with me

I will not allow it

Fullstop

It s not about the other person

I m doing that

I m kind of asking the other person to dump me so I can soak

Once again

Material for my art

Ok got it

I got it

And now what

I dont wanna

I don't wanna be like simon

Simon doesn't wanna be like simon

I don't mean the art part

Cos he or I wouldn't choose to be anything else

I mean the part with no money

With no tomorrow

Sadly enough

With no today

Mm

Stay with it

I can not forgive myself for letting my life slip away

That s why I m angry

That s what made me decide borrow this money off my mum

And desperation

But even they don't seem to grasp the situation in its entirety

I have no food

She suspects it though and she has told me

My dad is a bit more optimistic

I m looking at the view of my flat and I imagine I have built my own prison

Cant go anywhere today or can i

I mean I gonna have to

Not to say the day has to be a disaster

I could ask people come round bring some food

But who do I admit to that I haven't got any

And the weirdest thing is that it makes me kinda have to lie

And I hate lieing

I feel like I m cheating

I said

Am i trying to make u fall in love with me just to get u back?

No that would be terrible?

There is a sense of justice on that level

Only recently I decided to accept the view that I did go bouncing and rock climbing in order to get over ian

The rejection and the loneliness of seeing him in random moments kissing his girlfriend

It was a bit like hitchcok

I couldn't bare why it couldn't be me

I did ask

You see

And he did tell me later that he wasn't in love with me

He said it with conviction and a bit dry like no I wasn't in love with you

I think he must have added I was in love with Claire

Cos that s how I remember her name after all

Tragedy

Funny tragedy I don't know which came first- me or her

I know I kept coming all the way to the park and back the other day

Funny that

What kundalini energy can do

Life is based on it

I do need to switch off my phone again it pisses me off this is my therapy and I need this time…

Tryin to relate

Tryin to survive

I guess so

So I guess

My boyfriend decided to stay out tonite not tell me or text me

Ok

Fuck him

Why do I have to be forgiving

I don't want to be the person that breaks his balls but you know he could tell me something

Like goodnite baby sorry I didn't make it but I ll make it up to you

Fine

But nothing

Is like ok we don't need to do all that shit

Baby you r confusing me

I feel shit anyway I don't need you remember

Actually I m sick of allways allocating the problem to me

He could say sorry baby goodnite I couldn't make it tonite but I ll make it up to you

Or say nothing

I m fuckin bored of this shit

It was his idea to meet up at the first place

Dick

It s like I m not supposed to have any expectations

Fuck off

I m sorry I mean so little to you

I m sorry I feel like shit

I m sorry I m all stressed out for my interviews tomoro

Fuck off you twat

I just cant

I just can not be bothered

I can not

I shall not

I mean isn t it a good enough reason

I could do things but I cant be bothered

Why be so angry etc etc

It s a bit like hm well

I cant be bothered

I mean it

Seriously

Seriously im not sure about anything

I need a film to get lost in

I need some sleepers and a cup of tea

A sleepover

A sleep deprivation

I need stuff

I need everything indeed

I need it all

I need a life

I need some stuff from that vintage place in notting hill

I need to sort it out

I need it s seriously overdue

Due

I need food etc etc

I need my life

I m glad

I m glad I survived and I don't mean to glorify anything]

But think

Everything happens for a reason

And you know

Anyway I don't know anything

But

Loosen up

See what happens if you actually do

Things could be good for all of you

Apart

And all of you together

In any case at the moment you are just chilling

That s what you r doing

X 31 /10/12 a bit later

I m not dying

I m not dying to go anyway

And it s the risk that may be I get to spend time with the Chinese poo

Which I really don't think I can afford to take the risk honestly

It s just a bit too much isn't it

It s all a bit too much in fact

I hope she is somewhere with closer friends and family and she s speaking Chinese

I really don't know if she ll be there

Mm see what happens

It s that thing about the choice

I mean I don't know

It s fair or not fair to say that I could at least ask her via email so do u have any new years eve plans?

Cos I hope we aint got the same ones

Haha

It s just I can not stand the idea for a secont

So you know it s a bit tricky

I don't know what to say

I don't really like it

I don't really like any of it

And yohana and you know she s like my exes mate

I don't want to be shadowed by these people

I d rather fuck off to space

Innit

It s all good and everything but you know

I mean do u

I m sorry but

So

For whatever reason I didn't want fullon penetration

I wasn't sure

I was happy the way I was

As I said I am genuinely sorry I frustrated you

I would be happy if you had been able to come at that point I suppose just by rubbin ur cock on the outside of my vagina

Yes that s it

Equally you could have gone to the loo had a wank

I m angry at you cos u shouted at me but also cos u left in such a shockin manner- like- tvoux u disappear and shout at me

That creates an unwanted traumatic experience

I hate to dwell on my past but I had plenty of those

I m not gonna stay here be shouted at because I didn't feel like shagging

And even if I did I decided not to

It s my fuckin decision

If you feel there s no room for it look at it like that

Sometimes I d like us to go on- ie last nite- where in the end u wanted a nap

Fair enough I suppose- ur decision

I didn't start shouting or doing things

Anyway baby I don't want to have a fight over this I just want to set things straight

I m sorry as I said I frustrated you, that wasn't my intention

If you feel that when we start something we need to finish it we need to allow more time for that

And the fact is we don't have that sort of time in the morning-

I think it would be all right to give each other the benefit of the doubt in terms of when every kiss is going to end

I m sorry

I m sorry it didn't work my prescious pumkin

It wouldn't have had

Not with so much insecurity

Not with so many jokes

Not with so much time trying to kiss you

I mean

It got off to a bad start but actually now it s nearly over isn't it

I feel that it is and I m kind of cold and pre occupied

I feel this is too much for me to take and it kind of has to end

I cant

I can t deal with a situation it makes me uncomfortable and I feel utterly jealous

It wouldn't work I don't think

I cant take it I don't think

It s a bit too much

It makes me uncomfortable

I m sorry

It s too much

14/10/12

I think I

I think I wanted a boyfriend so much I didn't want to see how annoying he was

Do u remember when he was talking really loudly on the phone to Renato

I remember feeling embarrassed

Yet I decided to bypass it

Do u remember when I told him about wayne being slow

And he said

But I m like that

And I said no u r not

Well he is

He wasn't lying

He s slow and rooted and quite the opposite of me

The thing is they say the opposites attract

Really

Who said that

Like you kind a compliment each other

And appreciate each other

I feel a bit empty and spent

I want to be with simon

Cos he s dark and funny

And why did I ever stop

He wants to be with pippa

And fair enough

I don't expect to find love

I expect to find someone I want to be with

And then put my book in practice

And I thought that was Israel

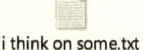
i think on some.txt

I ve come a long way

I feel I m going to explode

I don't feel comfortable any more

I returned the cards of my mum and dad and now on my own I don't feel that Israel is for me

He hasn't got the talent and the way to kiss me

He is indeed clumsy with his choice of flatmates

And I feel that I play a role in his life but he also needs to be honest about other people

Ie he s happy he says, he didn't know I felt so strongly about his flatmate

Ok now he does

See what he does

There s no more walks in the park as far as I m concerned

And anyway

I don't hate him but I could let him die

Could i

If I had to

No

7.10/12

It s all too much

I feel terrible

I ve been going through a tremendous amoun t of pain this week

There was this moment when sansan walked into the kitchen and I ve nefer felt so unwanted

I mean it was a chilling moment

The wasy she looked at me it was so like I wouldn't want to be there at all

I m scared of what may come

I m scared of the manipulateion I m not ready to confront or digest

I m interested in it as a social phenomenon but not so close to home

Anyway good luck to me andi feel really intimidated with the situation already

Internet without the hassle

Ok so what happened is I can actually work at my house at the mo

Cos I got internet

Yes I can

I can make the letters smaller and bigger

I can google pippa small oh dear

I can stalk simon

I can watch porn although I wont

I can go swimming in the lake

Fake

I can dive in the sun

Dip

I can just do fuck all

Fuck

I can just do

I can

Do

The light is too bright and the seat is too comfortable uncomfortable detrimental

Dunno

Must change it

And shaw I shoud

Shean

No it s sean

Ok what s the fuckin difference

In any case

I d like to see u

I like to lick you

I like to lick your balls

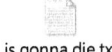
is gonna die.txt

It is now

Sun is shining

And I m looking out the window to work my relationship out

It needed work

And I alone didn't want to put it in

And my boyfriend is in a lazy mood

And I got lazy ovaries

That s not true

I got lousy unsupportive parents

And they are the hardest to confront

The one reason for not breaking up would be go to Greece and not have them break my balls

I can not tell them

It s none of their business

After all

It s all their fault

And yet again they ll look at me as if it s mine

Fuck that shit

No wonder they are alone without a daughter

I don't think they are that bad

But why do I think I am

Why

I m not bad for wanting to stay here in London without a daughter just myself

To nurture and to nourish

I need to look after my hair

What shall I do with my hair

I like my hair

Just let it be

It s time to stop

It s time to stop torturing myself

It s time to stop

Give it a go

Time has passed

Time will come by

With me in the same position

Of a drunk taxi driver

Driving a Chevrolet

Masseratti

Jaguar

Happy families

But why do u want to be drunk

Aren't you drunk enough

Haven't u had too much to drink

Too much too soon

Too soon too late

I mean really

Don't you feel sorry for yourself

Will you ever stop

Will you ever stop torturing yourself

You took yourself out of a relationship just as it was starting to work

You coulndn t deal with it

Truth is you still cant

You cant see why you should have another relationship while knowing the end

jeff

Perhaps no one put it better than Thomas Jefferson:

"Those,
which depend on ourselves,
 are the only pleasures a wise man will count on:
 for nothing is ours which another may deprive us of.

Hence the inestimable value of intellectual pleasures.

Ever in our power,
always leading us to something new,
never cloying,
 we ride serene and sublime above the concerns of this mortal world,
 contemplating truth and nature,
 matter and motion,
the laws which bind up their existence,
 and that eternal being who made and bound them up by those laws.

Let this be our employ.

Leave the bustle and the tumult of society to those who have not talents
 to occupy themselves without them."

Kai ti ekana

Fusika kai agxonomai

Den mu aresi o tonos tou kontou kais tin teliki ston idio tono tu apantisa

I mean u know

Kanonika tha eprepe na afxisi to noiki gia ton aprilio

Ah yes

Pernis narkotika agori mu

Exo epireasti ap ti seira pu vlepo

Nomizo oti ime I dalia

Alla imun ligo bitch me ton Israel

Giati

Den katalavaino

Giati me piese

Giati me piezoun olio

Prin kala kala m afisoun isixi theloun na me vgaloun ap to spitaki mu

I mean for the love of god

It s fuckin stressful

It s a beautiful house and I m a beautiful person

And it s not especially safe

And they re Indians and they know it

I ll go to the police and report our door downstairs

It s a little bit broken innit

It s a little bit strange

I don't feel great

I feel like hm dunno a bit apprehensive

Shall I take me out for a coffee in dalston

In homerton?

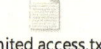
limited access.txt

lunchbreak

Many years of workplace research has clearly indicated that a failure to take a lunch break reduces personal effectiveness. Controlled studies indicate that assuming a worker arrives to work at 9.00am at 100% effectveness, without a lunch break by 5.00pm they are functioning at less than 35% effectiveness, however is the lunch break is taken the effectivenes at the end of the day is significantly above 50%.

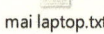
mai laptop.txt

Many people

Many people still believe women are just there to be fucked

And if they don't brag about it they actively demonstrate it

By throwing a tantrum dare she say no

Or

Is it just inevitable- in the spur of the moment they are genuinely just frustrated and they start shouting

Thing is I can imagine my mum being in the receiving end of this

Unable to say no she d be just sitting there willing to take it

Unforgiving to herself for being superior she s always curious about female orgasm

And so am I to an extend

I ll be reading lots of books and go to a sex therapist in the end of it all

Hope I don't break up with Israel but truth is I understand it to be a problem

And it s not a small problem as it s the source of every other break up or maybe it s causing it

Thing is if ur not connected at heart level it s kinda unbearable to feel the impact that has on ur sex life= and vice versa

Lets hope things work out for both of us together rather than individually

But i cant help but thinking that we may lose this battle hence each other

And I am really sorry

Me and john

http://en.wikipedia.org/wiki/Frog_%28horse%29

someone called hoof

and me called frog

come together

mm

also ian made me come on and on and what was that effect kundalini sexual energy live

life energy

dear god

I called him baby

I felt like my body was dissolving

Strange kindness from a man

And my pussy was so soft and wet and happy

And he does seem to enjoy it

I mean what is this

How

Does he

How does he feel

He says in the verge of orgasm

But he wont let me touch him too much in case he comes

I did want to lick his dick just lick it once

Ah the thought of it makes me throw my head back and I like that

I like ian

I liked looking at him and

Break-

Looking at his mouth while he was looking for me

Mistreating me

Streaming

How do I allow myself to be so fuckin overwhelmed by a fuckin computer

And why isn't it fuckin changing its letters when I said so

Why

Mm are you happy

Pop my cherries

Told mum and dad

Said it but in my own words

Daddy was really touched and really wanted to go

Really

It broke my heart to say what I had to say

That it was only on for one day the day I was there and then they were gone

Beautiful thing

But it s ok

He was happy

It really was the best I could do wasn't it

I mean under the circumstances

I mean you know what I mean

They are not conservative but I am their daughter

And they would be with me

I mean really

Not really

But I feel bad

He s my dad

And he wanted to be there in the biggest moment of my life

Is like I told them im secretly married

I mean

It s like that

I am sorry

I hope they understand

I hope they do

Mmm so frustrating

No fuckin way

Oo oo at least and at last

So yes I officially missed the fuckin deadline

And I feel like shit

But learn ur lesson

U would have felt like shit anyway

U would have found another reason

So yes baby since and u are for the moment a fitness trainer

It would be nice to do a course on computers oh no I mean trainer stuff

So u can get over urself and ur fears

And u know

U do doubt urself so much

Fuck that I m bored of doubting myself and you know I got to start a course in assertiveness

So yes when

M

When I m back

Great

#x

31 1 13

Mmm yoga

So thing is ye

I m not done my yoga yet

As of how I m hanging on

I read this book about man and dog

All I knew is already true

For instance you cant put pressure on ur dog to make u happy

So you cant to ur boyf

You cant rely on either of them to make u feel good about urself

Tricky

Also u have to seem un threatened

Remember for egsample Anastasia

And how u felt quite shit for her being in the same building blah blah

Anyway with Israel relationship was not healthy in so many ways

Aside from kissing

There were too many things wrong in fact

And to be honest I learnt from it

I learnt from that book

I need to make myself feel better

I need more money

I need a career of any sort

But first I need enough money to survive go partying traveling etc

Please it s time you did that now

Look after yourself properly

How

Do some more yoga

My book publishers

http://en.wikipedia.org/wiki/Semiotexte

my fuckin neighbours.txt

New everything

I m pretty much immobilised

Financially paralysed

I had a thought about the dosh and even so I m fucked or am i

Yes I am

I mean fuck

I just realized

Fuck

I ll have to check

I was gonna talk about men

I texted my dad

I don't like it

They force it upon me when they say they love me that I should love them too

I don't know what love is

It s complicated

Lets say I text it back out of politeness

In any case I was gonna talk about men

And how after the book I m able to understand them

Yes

That s something I realized when aged ten the bad boy of the school started hunting me down

After my mum s advice that I should play hard to get

up until that point I had just hunted him down I suppose

and then boom

the closest we ever got

I was laying down and he was laying on top of me

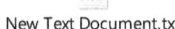
New Text Document.txt

Nice tip

"If you wish to achieve worthwhile things in your personal and career life, you must become a worthwhile person in your own self-development."

no but.txt

No I mean

Congratulations. She congratulates him on doing a good kus kus. Bloody Chinese you may well die, just imagine the whole of china, empty. Joy

No this is terrible, fantasies are terrible, and then oops a big rock hit the last one! Tvouz

Cartoon character, eyes on floor. Going straight. Get me. I never have come across a Japanese person I did not like.

Now I like Chinese food I guess but that doesn't say anything

We can still have british Chinese .

Like madagaskar,,,,

Like champagne and strawberries

Like tiramisu

And why black people have not heard of it

Why

I d lick his ass I ve had passionate sex with two black people

I m not a racist

Hm old argument#]

Anyhoo

What about simon

What about simon

What about simon

What about what about writing or just blathering

Writing for myself or writing for the world I cant decide

It doesn't work

It really really doesn't

I don't like it when I write to make sense

I don't want to make sense

Sensei

This is for me therefore

No really what

No real willingness to succeed

Ah as I d never be happy

As happy wasn't objective

Wasn't the objective

The aim

What was it

U don't try to slack u just work hard

Like a Chinese

And then die

Like a Lebanese

Of poverty

Like I m hungry now

Like I haven't eaten properly today

Thank god for the porridge

And you know

I could have had

I might have done

I mean what is it

What

Who

M

Boy George was saying I m more like me

And me too

I m more like me am i

Or I m so far ahead I can see myself coming

noo o.txt

Nothing ever prepares me

Baba se parakalo min kukloforis me to vraki su m enoxli

Might have done

Could have said

As Samantha puts it, men are like monkeys

They want to show it off

True

Samantha is what got me by in my darkest hours

I suppose it s something I have the choice to confront

Or to live with

Yes it bothers me

My dad was waiting for me to return his mobile half with his pants down

I mean why

What is there to see and why such hard work

And what goes through your head is the worse

I feel sorry for me and him

He thought of it

And I was surprised

Now about my thoughts and feelings

I feel hurt and sorry

And confused and angry and scared

Scared of what it may do to me

As a situation

What it may trigger what fuckin thougts and anger from the past transferred into the future

I don't want to fuck my future

O k so

There is a certain risk in the life I m living

Is t liver disease

Or chromosome incapacity

Or maladjustment

Or malnutrition

It s that mainly

It s the fact that no one not even me understands how broke I am

And I often try to neglect the fact that I m broken

But I mean I m getting to know me as we said

He spoke to me like I intended that

It was a fuckin accident

People die in accidents

You can be angry with me for making a mistake and causing an accident

But the truth is I am angry with yourself for lending me your favourite projector

And I am angry with myself for accepting it

I am also angry that although I considered it to be heavily heavy I still took it

I am angry I said to emma I have a projector when I clearly didn't

I am angry with the fact that I was going to bring a projector from London here and why

Why

I mean I really shouldn't

I should just say I fuckin hate to shit carrying stuff

And I m going to bricklane tomorrow first thing in the morning guess what carrying stuff

I am angry at the way I feel right now

And that I m so upset

Ok ime

Ime eroteumeni me to moro mu

Isn t it great

Den ime eroteumeni me to moro tis allis

As poume

I don't know

U know

It s a bit bizzare, when ur friend is not your friend etc etc- it s a bit like hm- what do u recon

Are you happy

Blazing happy

Blazing superstar happy

I mean

U can give up a friend for a doubt, a bad feeling a disbelief etc etc

U can decide u feel threatened by someone and give them up

Innit

I do think that actually, fair enough it could happen both ways

I mean fair enough

It s kinda like hm dunno

A bit bizzare

People don't expect it from me they don't see it coming

They don't expect me to be insecure

Ok and why – I just also feel that at some level idiosyncratically I don't work like that

I mean yes god damn im a mad

Like whorehopping= whaat???

I say shit god damn I m a man!!!!!! Should be fun

Ok so so

It seems to me that my therapist is pissed off with me and with him/

It s a tricky one

And me too for that countertransference

Who gives a fuck

I finally do

I actually do

I do give a fuck about me

That s good

And if that s how I feel= which I suspect it is

I am going to act on it

If he feels different

Let me know=- he will

But- in the end of the day, I need to do a few things on my own

Someone allocated me a therapist from the nhs a long time ago

And someone diagnosed me as depressed

A long time ago

And yes who gives a fuck= again and again

I think I need to make songs so it ll be like

Give me the tune I ll write you a song

What do u want it to be about

The tune?

The story of my life

Happy beatles

Happy families

Ok so the film

The film is gonna be like this

Anything and everything goes

The plot at the back is the story at the back of a dvd

I shall document more things such as my love life at the mo

Say a bit about orgasmic meditation

Look into it

Experiment with life

Life is an experiment

An experience

Make it fun

Make it last

Make it yours

I remember when tom – a rapist- told me how he felt about cheese

No I m just thrown a bit

Oh yes when he told me about tim that I respect him too much

When I do that I suppose I m in awe

I don't feel I want to play any more its more of a passive ahh

Do u remember when dan came in the room

I remember distinctly I wouldn't speak I would just sit there

And when I went for a drink with dan and tim I think in all accounts it was my dream team

But I was so into tim at that point, I was full with desire , explosive and exploring sex and inhibitions and falling in love and falling asleep in an expensive mattress

These were the days

I was incapable of forgiveness that s not ture

I had to forgive too much

But on the bright side sex was slow and tim was a great kisser

Ok so what have we got

What was the connection with my family

They did let me down

And I did let them down

So I feel that I m doing the same with society

If I stop letting myself down with society do u think I ll stop letting my parents down

Do u think If I stop for a second just stop stop

Just stop

What s it gonna be

The here and now

How long

How many years of therapy

How bizzare

I just cant do it any more

I feel sick actually

I feel this tremendous wave of sickness running over me

I feel I may be pregnant

In which case things will be different

And all together much more

But still

What the fuck

Am I supposed to take anything on or nothing at all or what

What is it that u want my little pumkin

I love you

So

Yes I keep letting them down and society down

But

Ok so

Dunno what do u recon

People break up all the time and all the time I feel like I m gonna break up

Thing is with people I don't really care about sex usually works

Say with simon it was just he was old there wasn t a threat of commitment of some sort or boyfriendhood

With tim I didn't wanna do it cos I hadn't enjoyed sex by that point

But I did cos I was melting while I looked at him

But we did spent all day in bed pretty much watching films hangin out the energy was building it was like foreplay

With Israel my foreplay time is limited and the cock starts trying to get into my pussy

He s not teasing me

He does it in real life maybe I should tell him that

He should do it in bed

But that requires thinking and he doesn't want to think

Ok

It s like a trivial like a puzzle

I don't think it s gonna work

I m trying to prepare myself for the possibility

I ll be crying for months whereas he ll be fine

Typical really

He ll be out having fun shagging people maybe or may be not

But that aint the point as he wont be shagging me

Dear old me

Ok still

So

He said

And I said

And he said

And it s all kinda in the air

One thing I read today

Everything I have done in my life so far have led me to this moment right now

I like it

It s a pretty good moment

I wish I don't split up with my boyfriend

I wish it s all a passing phase of exploring exploiting and exercising

The possibilities are endless

And this is somehow new knowledge

Is like a whole new book to a whole new chapter called my life

How funny

And it s about acceptance

And hiv positive

It s not funny any more

Life is not funny

Or is it

It s all a bit like hm dunno imimathia

Half learning

Better than non learning

What about what about Britney and kissing workshops and intimacy and fuckin tequila sunrise

What about sunset in santorini and clapping with the Chinese tourists

Fuckin Chinese

orgasm

So

As it happens

When it happens it apparently doesn't mean anything

Or so they say

Or so it seems

Or they don't know

Or whatever

But

When it doesn't happen

It ruins everything

So when it happens It doesn't fix anything

And when it doesn't happen it ruins everything

What is it

An orgasm!

Questions

In a relationship:

Haha

Oh well

Parapente text

Ine ligo ponokefalos to parapente ligo vavoura

Ine kai loipa kai loipa

Tora as pume ftiaxno to tsagaki mu kai tha to pio kai tha kano tin texni mu kai meta tha pao pros tas performance

I mean u know

Elpizo na min me xexasi o allos

Den to xexase apla u know

In any case

It s up to u

Up to me

Up to all of us

I love the fact that I m stretching more with a deadline ☺

I said every hour good idea

I m doing it now

23 3 13

Pes mu

Ime kourasmeni thelo na kimitho

Where is dick

Where

Where

I love dick

X

I am polyamoruous

But yoga says I m not

So how much egsactly do people want to pay for rent

And what were they thinking

I mean 130 pounds a week is a lot but we re in London and it s a nice flat

Innit

And I mean I really don't like his girlfriend and I really feel that she could be a threat

And I don't like him

It s a bit like hm I don't like to live with you in that energy

It s like hell in my opinion

He s tense and horrible and dark and he s been in the army

I mean why the hell do I want to live with him

And he fancies me and I don't trust him

So no is the answer

Sorry

Maybe I should tell him

No today

Innit

x

Plan be

- i also write stuff and am an artist as well, i want to know how to publish something and how to make it for sale as in your link- the basket purchase thing, i also teach yoga and i want something like that for a yoga class ie a purchase thing- i guess they are all very different, my main question was how to publish my writings/ print them, and have them available for sale - and then how to advertise them. auta

-
00:37
Anthony Anaxagorou

Ok. I'll be honest it's very hard selling you work if people aren't familiar with your material. The main problem I found when I started self-publishing in 2009 was that the only people who would buy my books would be family and friends. To really broaden your reader-base you will need to utilize both YouTube, social networks as well as live performances. You can set up an e-shop using Big Cartel to sell your products via a website but besides that it's still pretty difficult getting people to part with money, especially if it's something they haven't read or seen performed before.

-
00:40
Maria Tsartsali

mm interesting stuff- i think i should make a switch to some sort of stand up career now that i m still young- ish, and then carry the book with me. got a plan, thank you! still coffee if you like.

Pple I said no to

James Putnam

Mr serotta

psychanalisis

Very true too true, yes. And so . therefore. What would you like to say, what about, fuck that was heavy what about this justice what about Justin Hoffman what a bout what about,,, cheezy films, networking, teleporting, telesporting, lovelyhood , I mean, is it all about treating each other well.

And what does it mean

And why

Are you mean

You men

I can t generalize it

So my dad lets have it written

He again touched my chest with the back of his arm as soon as I got here

And when we had dinner he was looking at the mirror behind me

And yes he is acting upon it

And then he I saw him changing again.

Ok it s just that he s acting upon it

That s what the therapist says

Feelings are feelings is when u act upon them

Ok

But

Let s have it

I mean there is no reason to have no physical contact

But it has to be non perversive

And that s it

How do u do that

U do lots and lots and lots of yoga

And then I don't know pray meditate go to the beach

It s all part of a universal plan

read

A woman

A very interesting theory

Tear there

Second one:

Detach

I ve come a long way

Twin sista- is it trying

Would you say- the one with the shit

!! aand the winner is

cherries by xxx

i to r

the full works

I can sit down

I can sit down and have a little swim in my own poo

That's what I feel like

That s my next project

Reflections on the fourth of may 2013- no it s june

In may it was very different

In june it s like ha- im fuckin lovin it!

You know this artist that they made her paint the imprints on the wall because

Just because really

With no explanation

And you know no fuss she did it

Little did they know they were going to regret it so fast

I just got interrupted by my friend simon

Another big ego

So it s about big egos really isn't it

If I have one I hide it really well

I think that s why I like swimming in my own pool

So I mean really I mean I m enjoying the attention but to be honest

I mean really

What do u know

Little do they know about things

About life

No I don't want to be nasty and horrible

Some part of me anticipated that and I did think of that guy that had a whole de kiriko or Michael angelo room full of paintings and decided to paint over

But the thing is

Thennn

When the artist became famous and the art became valuable then the man had to pay shit loads to restore the space

There is something I felt listening to that story

I felt it s only fair

It s about the value of art

In money

It s about everything reflected in money that I despise

Money is our obsession and we are abusing each others lives in the name of money

I don't want anything to do with money

I guess I want money but it s a bit dramatic what we do for it

It s shame apparently

Shame is the only emotion that we have

And to be fair! Shame I mean- can take u places

I was thinking recently that it s the new levels of skint ness that I found myself into that drove me to pursue my career as a comedian

It s coming up

It s a barrier and you break through it

You live with shame

You don't try and hide it

It s also my art ie my pussy on the big screen

How satisfying

I mean really! I mean come on! I mean forget it!

I mean I m loving it!

London 4 june 2013.

I cant overestimate

The power of words

The power of cold

The power of knowledge

The power of so cold knowledge

The power of you and me

On the sofa

The power so far

The power so far ahead

The power so far ahead up your ass

The power of an umbrella

The power of you and me

The power the power the power of not being dyslexic

The power of running ahead knowingly

Not knowingly

The power of not knowingly

The power of you and me

The power of who u like

To be

M

The power of you and me

M

The power of mixtrust and new emotions

The new me

The new you and me

The power of light

The light

The power of dreams

H and m

Like h and d

Like Honda

1 3 13

I dont feel continue

Ok so am I really showing this piece

I mean am i

I mean I should

I mean it s a thought

A scary thought

Somehow harmless if you consider the physical body to be one that dies anyway

In the grand scheme of things it s not a massive gesture anyway

Would you say it would be classed as a jealous type of crime

But why

We allocate things ruthlessly allover the place

I m looking for the word

Senselessly, authaireta/ mmm I ll look it up

What do you know

What do u know

My friend simon is the only guy I know that actually tried to kill someone

By giving him lots of heroin

I felt priviledged he told me the story and I could totally see where he s coming from

My friend simon is someone I respect and love and I would forgive anything anyway

Socrates had said that "geniouses should be allowed to blabla and scandalise their uncles"2

Socrates was a pretty cool guy I presume with lots of time on his hands for spiritual cultivating1

Bit like gardening

Today,m he would live in essex in a villa, his son would be a plumber and he himself would have grown out of the roofer s business, with a profound mindfulness acquired from doing

As opposed to non doing

Yoga says: if you feel down, shit, frustrated, throw yourself into selfless service,,,

mmm. interesting, yoga to me is like an uncle that knows what he s talking about

but I may still choose to do the wrong thing

ah and there is no right or wrong anyway

just more and more complicated

to the point of simple

so can we just chill or go back to the crime

my nails are red

they are painted with the blood of this weekend

blood I wish I could draw

but I couldn't

I need to express more in time

Or make a strategy

A plan

A train in stratford

Stratford express,,,,,,,,,,,

I aint gonna kill anyone so that s a good start

That doesn't stop me from dreaming about it

And you know

It s not a nightmare

Nanait

1. Spiritual cultivation

2. George Bernard Shaw (1908:19) who observed that since the nature of genius is such that it is usually in conflict with some institution that is 'far behind the times', 'it is necessary for the welfare of society that genius

should be privileged to utter sedition, to blaspheme, to
outrage good taste, to corrupt the youthful mind, and,
generally to scandalize its uncles...'

I dont feel

Comfortable with that coment

;; it s not fair – you got a girlfriend it s not fair;;

I would feel less comfortable if you swallowed your tongue

Bit more comfortable if the bone of your nose went into your brain

Is it too much to ask

Why

Why do we classify crimes so unfairly

I d like to see the end of your nose sticking out through the back of your head

Now I feel better, good, now I can say I can let that one go

But not now

As this hasn't happened yet

I m telling you – people die

All the time

It s not fair

Why is it not fair

I think it s not fair I m not allowed to stick the fork in your eye

And I think I m right

And you know justice is a big joke an entrepreneur s business anyway

Oh sweet

This is the material for my Halloween nite

Hallo ☺

I dont know once again

What just happened

I set my own boundaries

I explained my point of view

I gave options

And it backfired

What about what about

What about how I feel

Once again

Ok mum

Hi mum

Mum?

#you have got to be an idiot

And I get it

It s just I don't want to be with an idiot

You cant be an idiot if you re with me

And in the end of the day it s all come clear

You can t be with me

I will not allow it

Fullstop

It s not about the other person

I m doing that

I m kind of asking the other person to dump me so I can soak

Once again

Material for my art

Ok got it

I got it

And now what

Let s just say

I m happy and sad

X

14/10/12

What do u think

Make or break

Black or white

Anti yoga

It s all been done over and done with

But to be honest

His flatmate teaching him piano

I mean

There has to be a line

I m not clear about it

I feel insecure and all

I feel violated and betrayed

Untrusty

Unworthy

Of love

Of commitment

Of any sort of explanation

I feel that it s kind of again in need of lots of work

Ok baby tell u what

When ur flatmate chanchan is teaching you piano

I ll be there

I mean ok

We can flirt

We can have friends

And I can have orgasmic meditation with ian

And watch films with simon

Ok lets do that

Lets make each other unhappy with our behaviour

Lets why not

Why

Ah because we know

We know a bit better

But maybe we don't

Has it crossed your mind

We don't know any better

We re just like anybody else

Trying to live our lives as best as we could

I ll be an artist all the way

And you be flirty be shitty knock yourself out

Just don't bother me

Elo s friend

What do u do

I mean

Distractions

As tony put it we get carried away all the time

All the time

I find it a bit boring

It is a bit boring

I can make the stupid sculptures and go to india

Can t i?

I mean can t i?

With a note

I exist

Make me famous and we ll both get rich

At least you are

So speak soon

Kind regards

Thickandtastyxxx

Mmmmmmmmmmm yummie

Door knocker

Called

Knock yourself out

X

Going in our out of the house

It doesn't matter

If you live in hackney you may want to put it on the inside

If you live in hamstead outside would be good

Although really

If people see you they will call the police

And if it s stupid fuckin expensive and they re junkies they ll take the risk

Mmm

I am actually happy

I feel that we had sex twice and it actually worked

And we did also have had a near snog experience

Not quite worked yet

But hey

I feel that we did close some sort of circle

Just as he let his guard down

I took him down

That s very much what I do

That s very much what has happened to me

I teach people to not trust me

And I learn not to be trustworthy though my behaviour

And not trust people either

M

So what was that about acceptance

It s like

If you accept other people you will accept yourself

It s like if you accept people going to the zoo

You will accept yourself for instance what

Doing what that I feel is so cruel

Not feeding my plant

But to my defense I didn't want a plant at the first place

I wouldn't get one as I know am in no position to look after it

Right

I mean I like them but haven't bought one

I just said to someone on the phone that I broke up with my boyfriend

It s a new level of pain

Quite familiar but also different because I actually did think that this is the real thing

But really it was too much

It was too intense and too consuming

I don't think I want to be with him at this point

I don't want to have to feel threatened by his flatmate, by his style and his bodylanguage towards her and me and the situation

I m bored of flirting boyfriends and I can say that it really honestly and utterly it was for the best

Or can i

Can i

I mean really I don't know

I don't think it s fair the way I m made to feel

I mean really

Am I spoiled

I don't think so

It s the first time I take myself seriously

I don't want to be with someone that makes me feel uncomfortable about his flatmate

And I mean

Why

Am I not supposed to be able to communicate those feelings

Am I not supposed to be myself

Am I not supposed to be all right

I m a little bit bored

A little bit distressed

And a little bit unhappy

But only a little bit

It s a little bit

I don't want to be with him

Remy said I m trying to be someone that I m not

He means square

And boring

And monogamous

But what if I am all these things and many more

What I m not is

Not able to cope with competition

Not cut to feel threatened or uncomfortable

I retaliate

And yes you know

Shit happens it s a bit like hm what do u know

I ve been raped by my friends

I ve been abused by my parents

And it s all gone down a treat

I took it on the chin like Barbie would do

Knocking her door knockers

Years of abuse produce years of abusive behaviour

Towards myself and towards others

Isn t it

It s all inter related

On the bright side

I let my dog down in the end

But not during at least not when I was with her

So yes there is a spectrum of behaviour and a possibility of change

It s just not dynamic and it s not overnite

It s gradual and sometimes you die during

Scary shit

I dont wanna

I don't wanna be like simon

Simon doesn't wanna be like simon

I don't mean the art part

Cos he or I wouldn't choose to be anything else

I mean the part with no money

With no tomorrow

Sadly enough

With no today

Mm

Stay with it

I can not forgive myself for letting my life slip away

That s why I m angry

That s what made me decide borrow this money off my mum

And desperation

But even they don't seem to grasp the situation in its entirety

I have no food

She suspects it though and she has told me

My dad is a bit more optimistic

I m looking at the view of my flat and I imagine I have built my own prison

Cant go anywhere today or can i

I mean I gonna have to

Not to say the day has to be a disaster

I could ask people come round bring some food

But who do I admit to that I haven't got any

And the weirdest thing is that it makes me kinda have to lie

And I hate lieing

I m not keen on it at all

I feel that this hurts most the whole impression management

And the fact I live in London people do all sorts of things to piss me off

Ie they work hard, make money, rub it in, they say things like "I bought a whole packet of yoga classes and it expired, if it makes u feel better". Does it? In a way I suppose I understand it s hard for people to commit to themselves and go through with their planned things as I guess life catches up. I have no life. I have nothing, or so I say to myself as I need to get out of here as soon as possible. I can t be like this. I m organising a yoga class for tomorrow, see what happens, I ll invite some more people today,,,

In theory I was gonna go to a carboot today, in practice I couldn't afford it. Oh well. It would have been much more fun going with someone as well. Hm. Strangely familiar. Everything would have been more fun going with someone. But it seems I have no one to tag along be best mates with and the people that I know I need to be able to afford things with. So I cant go for a drink like normal people and when I do I can never and I mean never buy a round.

And I m not a junkie, at least in the real sense. I am in the deeper sense of abusing myself or not knowing how to treat me right. I hit the nail on the head. Cos that s how I was brought up, and that s the problem with Israel, and many of my relationships in the past. And that s why I stopped having them. It s interesting , cos I see there is a fault in the way I treat myself, I decide not to have anyone treating me like I treat myself, and anyone that treats me better I can not handle, anyone that treats me equally (bad, awkward, inappropriately), I feel rightly so I shouldn't have a relationship with, including myself. With myself though I can t run away literally, I can split like a split personality, I can shut me out and punish me, stop feeding me and never pay my taxes. Result!

But it ll get sorted out, I m dealing with it, the other thing is para pente, a series that I watch obsessively over and over and I pretend I m dalia, the good hearted rich kid. Lets have some of that! But it s sunny outside and there s life out there indeed… I mean, what shall I do?

13 4 13

I feel like I m cheating

I said

Am i trying to make u fall in love with me just to get u back?

No that would be terrible?

There is a sense of justice on that level

Only recently I decided to accept the view that I did go bouncing and rock climbing in order to get over ian

The rejection and the loneliness of seeing him in random moments kissing his girlfriend

It was a bit like hitchcok

I couldn't bare why it couldn't be me

I did ask

You see

And he did tell me later that he wasn't in love with me

He said it with conviction and a bit dry like no I wasn't in love with you

I think he must have added I was in love with Claire

Cos that s how I remember her name after all

Tragedy

Funny tragedy I don't know which came first- me or her

I know I kept coming all the way to the park and back the other day

Funny that

What kundalini energy can do

Life is based on it

I do need to switch off my phone again it pisses me off this is my therapy and I need this time…

Tryin to relate

Tryin to survive

As I was sayin before but wasn't that explicit with ian was that it s like trying to wee without a fart

I mean u know u can do it

Almost

Nearly

But then it s missing the point isn't it

Why should you deprive yourself from this moment of indulgence and satisfaction

Who is more important than that

It s shame

The only feeling in the world that we got

And I have a lot to do with shame

I m fighting it with all my weaknesses

And my vulnerability is my only strength

Yes I don't mind being vulnerable

I may even be cheating on myself

I may be a calculative bitch that s trying to get him back

As in you know even –

I may be playing chess with my chest all the way to the bank

And after all

Who s got a flair for writing

If only me

If only I could be bothered

I need to find my phone and switch it off

I mean what was that with ian before

I was thinking

I was a lot in my head

And that s probably after teaching a couple of yoga classes

And that s also after trying to work out my performance

And that s also after bumping into jonathan wanting to ask him if he wants to do my performance in his gallery…

Mmm I think I d like him to for a change come to me

I think that s how I ll do it

But I could ask him first

I could

Nothing to hide

Literally x

I am a savvy business woman and that is a role close to heart

I ve always thought of money as style

And I think that s why they start to annoy me cos they cramp my style if I don't have it

And also cos you know I want to have sex with ian

But I m thinking of sean

Another bad egssample

What the fuck was this about

It s typical of men to try and detatch from the situation once they re not running after us

It s a lot of come and go and a lot of run and chase

Today I m not going anywhere

I m here to stay

I may do this performance in the tate at the big room

Why not

Like a virgin.

Can u see it

Or in bloody serpentine…

But I mean can I do it as part of my degree show lets say and then you know take it outside…

I guess so

So I guess

My boyfriend decided to stay out tonite not tell me or text me

Ok

Fuck him

Why do I have to be forgiving

I don't want to be the person that breaks his balls but you know he could tell me something

Like goodnite baby sorry I didn't make it but I ll make it up to you

Fine

But nothing

Is like ok we don't need to do all that shit

Baby you r confusing me

I feel shit anyway I don't need you remember

Actually I m sick of allways allocating the problem to me

He could say sorry baby goodnite I couldn't make it tonite but I ll make it up to you

Or say nothing

I m fuckin bored of this shit

It was his idea to meet up at the first place

Dick

It s like I m not supposed to have any expectations

Fuck off

I m sorry I mean so little to you

I m sorry I feel like shit

I m sorry I m all stressed out for my interviews tomoro

Fuck off you twat

I m sorry I have a shit boyfriend that is so tight and doesn't give a shit

I think I m selling myself low here

Fuck you

I ll go dating

good

I just cant

I just can not be bothered

I can not

I shall not

I mean isn t it a good enough reason

I could do things but I cant be bothered

Why be so angry etc etc

It s a bit like hm well

I cant be bothered

I mean it

Seriously

Seriously im not sure about anything

I need a film to get lost in

I need some sleepers and a cup of tea

A sleepover

A sleep deprivation

I need stuff

I need everything indeed

I need it all

I need a life

I need some stuff from that vintage place in notting hill

I need to sort it out

I need it s seriously overdue

Due

I need food etc etc

I need my life

I need a snakeskin jacket

And a rough magazine

I need a life of luxury and a Mercedes bens

And a flight to paris

A train to paris

And a b a ticket

And a basket

And nuts

And fruits

And a magazine

I need magazines in order to tailor make them cut and paste them make a salad and an adult education magazine

Things you should know

Things I should know

A year in paris

What is it

What do u want

Shall I go to san Francisco

Shall I live and die

Shall I boob fight

For whatever reason I can t be bothered

Lathered

I mean seriously

Dustin Hoffmann is talking some sense

There is not a lost opportunities aa group now is there

Would I lead it

Not so much

Kindo f yes so much some times

A little bit

A bit

Quite a bit

A lot

Fuck

I mean

Or maybe I know

I know nothing

I know too much

Too much

It can never be too much

I know how the world works

The world order

And I ve lost faith in life

Have i

Not it s not the same

I have faith in life

I don't have faith in how the world works

On a human approach

On a human relations

I m not sure about humans

I m sure about life

Life blood

Life scene

Life

I got to see more trees

More nature

I have to leave London once a week

I never listen

Oh do i

I mean really

What do u recon

Like there s no tomorrow

X

18 12 12 second text

I m glad

I m glad I survived and I don't mean to glorify anything]

But think

Everything happens for a reason

And you know

Anyway I don't know anything

But

Loosen up

See what happens if you actually do

Things could be good for all of you

Apart

And all of you together

In any case at the moment you are just chilling

That s what you r doing

X 31 /10/12 a bit later

I m not dying

I m not dying to go anyway

And it s the risk that may be I get to spend time with the Chinese poo

Which I really don't think I can afford to take the risk honestly

It s just a bit too much isn't it

It s all a bit too much in fact

I hope she is somewhere with closer friends and family and she s speaking Chinese

I really don't know if she ll be there

Mm see what happens

It s that thing about the choice

I mean I don't know

It s fair or not fair to say that I could at least ask her via email so do u have any new years eve plans?

Cos I hope we aint got the same ones

Haha

It s just I can not stand the idea for a secont

So you know it s a bit tricky

I don't know what to say

I don't really like it

I don't really like any of it

And yohana and you know she s like my exes mate

I don't want to be shadowed by these people

I d rather fuck off to space

Innit

It s all good and everything but you know

I mean do u

I mean dunno

Isn't it??

What do u recon

The chances are just not there

But you know what about elo

What if she decides to come and bring the shit with her

I do have a real problem is that bad

If there is one person on the planet I d rather not be together this new years is that fuckin shit

And I don't think I can afford the risk as I m generally a little out of shape emotionally

Mm

Ok then

Do what u got to do

27 12 12

I m sorry but

So

For whatever reason I didn't want fullon penetration

I wasn't sure

I was happy the way I was

As I said I am genuinely sorry I frustrated you

I would be happy if you had been able to come at that point I suppose just by rubbin ur cock on the outside of my vagina

Yes that s it

Equally you could have gone to the loo had a wank

I m angry at you cos u shouted at me but also cos u left in such a shockin manner- like- tvoux u disappear and shout at me

That creates an unwanted traumatic experience

I hate to dwell on my past but I had plenty of those

I m not gonna stay here be shouted at because I didn't feel like shagging

And even if I did I decided not to

It s my fuckin decision

If you feel there s no room for it look at it like that

Sometimes I d like us to go on- ie last nite- where in the end u wanted a nap

Fair enough I suppose- ur decision

I didn't start shouting or doing things

Anyway baby I don't want to have a fight over this I just want to set things straight

I m sorry as I said I frustrated you, that wasn't my intention

If you feel that when we start something we need to finish it we need to allow more time for that

And the fact is we don't have that sort of time in the morning-

I think it would be all right to give each other the benefit of the doubt in terms of when every kiss is going to end

As it would really be impossible to do otherwise

If at the same time u feel like you are getting bloodshots running through ur head at times like this morning maybe then try and keep all this in mind and find out for yourself how u wanna handle it

Love you lots

maria

I m sorry

I m sorry it didn't work my prescious pumkin

It wouldn't have had

Not with so much insecurity

Not with so many jokes

Not with so much time trying to kiss you

I mean

It got off to a bad start but actually now it s nearly over isn't it

I feel that it is and I m kind of cold and pre occupied

I feel this is too much for me to take and it kind of has to end

I cant

I can t deal with a situation it makes me uncomfortable and I feel utterly jealous

It wouldn't work I don't think

I cant take it I don't think

It s a bit too much

It makes me uncomfortable

I m sorry

It s too much

14/10/12

I think I

I think I wanted a boyfriend so much I didn't want to see how annoying he was

Do u remember when he was talking really loudly on the phone to Renato

I remember feeling embarrassed

Yet I decided to bypass it

Do u remember when I told him about wayne being slow

And he said

But I m like that

And I said no u r not

Well he is

He wasn't lying

He s slow and rooted and quite the opposite of me

The thing is they say the opposites attract

Really

Who said that

Like you kind a compliment each other

And appreciate each other

I feel a bit empty and spent

I want to be with simon

Cos he s dark and funny

And why did I ever stop

He wants to be with pippa

And fair enough

I don't expect to find love

I expect to find someone I want to be with

And then put my book in practice

And I thought that was Israel

And that love is is significant

My significant other

He s a good friend

With a Chinese girlfriend

The truth is I feel manipulated and mis used

By myself

By anyone

By everyone

I m going to Greece for four days

And I expect to sink into food and laughs

I love my life after all

And you know what

My baby doesn't deserve me right now

He tried to please me and he failed

I mean lets face it

He doesn't want to win

And he wont

He doesn't want to be with me

And that s why it hurts so much

He was waiting couldn't believe I changed so much became so pleasant overnight

Why did i

Cos I knew he d leave

And I wanted to make it difficult for me

And for him

But also I hoped to give it another go

But he cant kiss me

He failed

We failed

Together

We got to learn to explore to be patient

But all these kissless moments took their toll

I m sorry

X

20.11.12

I think on some

level i d like to kill myself
i m not going to- for sure- u never know but-
and on some level i already am
why else am i here sulking, hungry, while i could be
shagging
or having fun
as i forget shagging is about having fun
simon yes simon or a period of my life i was lucky
now i m not
ok got to live with it
it s just i m not feeling it- is it possible- but sometimes it works
when i m in charge- when were playing...
see what happens
im happy and sad
i m sad
and guilty for it- i cant sustain a negative emotion i feel guilty for
it
fuckin be sad sad fuck off
but ok i plead guilty for letting god down
everything down
me, my boyfriend- what the fuck - i dont know- i feel shit so shit it s
understandable that s the saddest thing
it s understandable
and you are wrong
and you are fucked up and u always will be
and there is nothing you can do about it
it s all gone wrong-
why not
fuck off
i m flat 8
isnt it funny how- how oh how i m flat 8
i m flat
and i m eight
i feel so sad and angry and sad and sad
and i wanna cry till i die
what do u want
im just saying
why dont i leave me alone to feel all these things
it s all too much of a disappointment to take in in one ge
i m upset out of balance sad in a bad mood cold and hot and bothered
i feel sulky and i feel i m being rude to my boyfriend the only one i
want
and its sad- i m suicidal and i wont do it i cant do it but- i could
jump out the window
i could n t do it to my family
could n t do it to my mum and dad
i m really really sorry
but i could do it to me to little maria
dont i love her a bit more
can i really make it look like an accident
i mean really
seriously

i m premensural and depressed- i ll go to a solicitor cos part of the
problem is that i cant get in and out of the house
because of the lights- yes the fuckin lights- they scare me

they fuckin do
i hate it i fuckin hate it
all right i ll go to a solicitor- fuck them-

I ve come a long way

I feel I m going to explode

I don't feel comfortable any more

I returned the cards of my mum and dad and now on my own I don't feel that Israel is for me

He hasn't got the talent and the way to kiss me

He is indeed clumsy with his choice of flatmates

And I feel that I play a role in his life but he also needs to be honest about other people

Ie he s happy he says, he didn't know I felt so strongly about his flatmate

Ok now he does

See what he does

There s no more walks in the park as far as I m concerned

And anyway

I don't hate him but I could let him die

Could i

If I had to

No

7.10/12

It s all too much

I feel terrible

I ve been going through a tremendous amoun t of pain this week

There was this moment when sansan walked into the kitchen and I ve nefer felt so unwanted

I mean it was a chilling moment

The wasy she looked at me it was so like I wouldn't want to be there at all

I m scared of what may come

I m scared of the manipulateion I m not ready to confront or digest

I m interested in it as a social phenomenon but not so close to home

Anyway good luck to me andi feel really intimidated with the situation already

But why

U r not good enough to tell her to fuck off

Listen I see what u r toint and I cant be botheeed

I m sorry for you wether you get what u want or not it s not the point

I have much to lose but in the big picture u may lose a hand in the tube

Or a leg

Or both

And anyway I hope you do anyway

Is that too much to ask

Why

And arm and a leg

7.10.12

Internet without the hassle

Ok so what happened is I can actually work at my house at the mo

Cos I got internet

Yes I can

I can make the letters smaller and bigger

I can google pippa small oh dear

I can stalk simon

I can watch porn although I wont

I can go swimming in the lake

Fake

I can dive in the sun

Dip

I can just do fuck all

Fuck

I can just do

I can

Do

The light is too bright and the seat is too comfortable uncomfortable detrimental

Dunno

Must change it

And shaw I shoud

Shean

No it s sean

Ok what s the fuckin difference

In any case

I d like to see u

I like to lick you

I like to lick your balls

What if I changed the letter

Sent it

I changed the seat

Seriously now

What if

I would say

I love you

Do u want to be with me and fuck me every day

Deep and slow

Would you say yes

Is that romantic

That takes the bone and sticks it far away from us

Truth is I believe the story with the bone

And I need to cut myself and bleed over it whilst reading it so I don't forget

And meditate over it

And yes

Truth is it hasn't got me anywhere in terms of sean

But also truth is I m still learning it

It s a new technique

It s a new day

But I m feeling good

So what am I gonna do

I mean really

Why am I so slow and hard to get

With eric

With sean

I want him to chase me

So I ll have to chase myself

More work

More texts

It goes like that

I ll come to ur hood tomorrow with a boy from Greece where would you say it s the coolest place to blow his mind?

That s aggressive

He ll say fuck off what do u want

No that s what I d say

He ll say I don't know superdrug

Or café otto

Isn't that a bit heavy

Isn't it a bit mean

I cant do it

If he says I don't know

What do I say

I don't mind

Miss u sean

I can say sthin like

U can meet me too it should be fine

It s not a too bad msg coming to think about it

Is it

I don't know

He may say come over if you want and u can blow my mind

Haha

I want to tell him I want to have a drink or a tea with him tomorrow

I can come in the morning for a cup of tea in the area so it motivates me to wake up?

Sean are u happy are u asleep

Are u happily asleep

Send him that and then lots of kisses xxxx

What do u recon

What do u recon

What do u recon

What do u recon

What do u recon

What do u recon

Blow your mind

Blow your mind

Blow you away

Blow me up

Blow job

Blow his mind

Yes you know somewhere exotic

In dalston

Dalston is an exotic shithole

Blow my mind out of the blue shithole

Would you say u know people are buying flats

For fucks sake

I mean

What can I say

Walthamstow

Anywhere really

How people buy flats I do not know

Sean is saving money renting his place

I had an offer and blew it again

What can I say

Really

I mean

You know

What s the story

Telling

The story telling

You and me

I mean I should shouldn't i

I don't have enough money to survive or pay the rent

I at least should take the fuckin tax credit

Yes do please

Do please

Do

Please

Do please

Do please

Please do

Don't know

I m stressed and freaked out

But why

Cos I cant afford to pay the rent this month

And it s not looking good at any rate

Is it

I mean really now

Fuck

I mean really

Now fuck

Fuck now

Fuck

Ok so sell my prints

Sell my tits

I couldn't even do that

But why do u say that babe

U understand it s all to do with positive reinforcement

I mean do u

I mean u do

I mean u should

I mean u do

It s like that

U put ur stuff online on the Saatchi page

And it says prints

Yes

Ten pounds a print

Yes tenner

A print yes

Good

Now

What the fuck

U gonna do

Get a stall in Brixton and sell them for a tenner

Or take them somewhere in broadway market

Tenner

And vintage clothes

Or just art

Tenner

You recon

Where else

Oh dear yes bloody galleries of course

Tenner

Tate

Tenner

I mean really maria if only you had a fuckin product

To sell

Tenner

You d be rich you understand

Tenner

And thickandtastyxxx is ready for that

Tenner

Please maria just do it babes

And why is my name underlined

Cos it s with a small letter u fool

You should be up there

But you must

You should is a word full of guilt

And must is an obligation

The question u need to ask urself is do u want to

Are you scared that ur parents will rip you off

And take u down and rip you apart like old newspaper

Wallpaper

Old news

Yes I m scared

And that s what it s all about

It s still the same

You cant allow yourself success at this point more than ever

Or can you

You need some help

What about that woman with the heart Rosenberg method

She ll give u three free sessions

But u weren't ready

But now u are

Good boy

Good girl

Smells like dee jay

Here we go

August

Snog

Snog

Oh

He did rip u apart when he said u want something from me don't you

That s when u weren't throwing him the bone

You were just keeping it for yourself

Now you would know what to do

You would throw it back

Out there

Out there

Out there

I can blow your mind any time of the day mr sean

Any fuckin time I can blow your mind in flying colours

Blow it

Blow it let me

I ll text u the aggressive text

Shall i

Xxxxxxxxx

I ll blow your mind

Your mind

I ll have to blow your mind before I blow anything else from the looks of it

But u are sensitive

And you know

I told you that I cant come up cos I ll want to fuck you

And you said you silly you made me think about us with that text

That was me being me back then

That s what I like

And that s egsactly what I don't like when im training men

Like dogs

That I train me first

It s a lot of self discipline

No one talks to you about that

 You need to train urself to be a trainer

Ha

But it pays off

Apparently

The reason that text was memorable was cos I said no in the end

That s why he thought

Because the bone was out there

I can t come to ur house I said

Cos I ll wanna fuck u

And I shouldn't

Ffuuoui

Criss crossing through the air

Through the sky and the leaves

All the way to the moon

And back

And we re back

About tomorrow yes it s like that a bit

A bit like I want to blow someone else s mind and you cant come

Or maybe u can

I don't know

You know

He s not that into me

Innit

It s true

Isn't it

When did he say he thought I like him

I cant even remember

When

And why

I mean when and why

He said I thought I m in on a random occasion

Really

For me it was then under the bridge

When I touched his arm

And then couldn't stop thinking about it

And then I said to him that I d need to do some work tonite but soon

Bone

Bone bone

I love it because I was playing the game unknowingly

Really and utterly honestly

But even now I make me proud for trying

Blow your mind

Blow my mind

Oh

Shall I have some saki

I mean

I mean

I had a few quite sad moments

With san san a few misunderstandings a few mis alignments

A couple of great shags of course

And I m still horny

I still feel we could have the best sex with Israel right now

But he wants it to be love

Ok whatever

Maybe I m not ready to move on yet

May be that s why the wait

The hold

On seans part

What does he want to know

Do I have to tell him that I broke up with my boyfriend

Do i

I mean do i

Do i

I probably need to break up first

Someone said they feel it

But I did tell him that it s our first date

And you know

I had neck marks

On my neck

Yes that s true he likes to bite

Bite

But when sex is good it doesn't matter

I mean he doesn't have to

I mean I d love to see him

And bite him

And kiss him

And look at him

I cant even look at him

I feel too overwhelmed

It s funny

I feel too horny to even look at him

I really fuckin want him

I feel I may fuck eric just cos I want sean so much

But not just shag sean

Make me feel beautiful

Make him come here

And then u can fuck

Like there s no tomorrow

It s too much

Its tonite

Tonite

It s a bit too much tonite isn't it

It s a bit too much isn't it

I mean I m so skint

The thing is

I m so super skint I could sell the over locker

I mean really I could

And the other one

I m not using them it s true

What about my baby laptop

I m kinda using it aren't i

Well yes

What about

My prints

Oh please

Just my prints

And what about some workshops in my house

Like hm creativity workshops

Or yoga workshops

Or what

I ll look into that dance of yoga thingy

You want it

x
3/1/13

Is gonna die

and is gonna be my fault
actually not
actually its life it s nobody s fault
actually we re all gonna die
actually why dont we die today
tonite
before my interview
i feel sorry for my parents
they ll die with me or even better they wont have the strentgh to die
they ll be like it was all our fault
actually my life
right now
it s my responsibility
and i have to live it the way i want to
so maybe be a stripper
maybe disappear
maybe go to the moon
maybe just die in my sleep
but got to be said it s my decision
and i am my liability
thank you

so with art therapy
i give me the dignity to cure myself
haha
i can relive my own childhood
how long about ten years or sixteen
yes a lifetime
i want to die more than i want to live
and that is actually not true
i really want to live but i m not
i havent got the skills
i need to be spontaneous and impulsive
i need to feel that the other person is there with me
i hate to feel that i m pestering them to come along
i never do
i actually never do
it s not nice
i feel sick
i wanna die

i wanna sell my clothes cut my hair etc etc

i feel sick and lonely
what do u do

i mean what do u think you can do
really
i feel like i ve emptied my soul i told israel what a shit week i had
and i expressed the need to say goodbye
but no
he s a solid rock
he wont move an inch
ok and to get him back i wanna break up with him

yes
i mean it will take a while to actually re build my life but
i didnt in any way change it so should be fine
i mean really- who cares - honestly
i m not ready i dont think we r right for each other
i dont think i m right for anyone for fuck s sake

who am i kidding and why am i lying to myself and anybody else
i m a kid
i need pampering and i mean to be fair my family makes me feel really uncomfortable
i eat pussy
i think i wanna tell them that

i actually dont really know how to break it to myself but i hate people too much to be with anyone

i just cant deal with them
i m gonna sell my phone for fifty quid- and that s it
i m gonna sell my clothes a pound each on a carboot on sunday
and my luis vuitton bag for twenty quid
and a couple of pairs of shoes for ten quid
so i ll have a hundred pounds from them all
and a hundred i got left from mum and dad that s two hundred
and thirty from elisa from trousers that s all i ll spend on the wkd
so on monday i ll go to goldsmiths with two hundred pounds
also i can rent my room for a hundred a week from next week= it s all happening
good on you mate
things will be fine

plus i ll start working
plus i ll tell the guy that i think i ll break up with my boyfriend and it s ok because i ll be a lesbian but very very happy
i think i want to date girls
i think i ll join a lesbian tantric sex site
why not
i mean i m bored anyway

It is now

Sun is shining

And I m looking out the window to work my relationship out

It needed work

And I alone didn't want to put it in

And my boyfriend is in a lazy mood

And I got lazy ovaries

That s not true

I got lousy unsupportive parents

And they are the hardest to confront

The one reason for not breaking up would be go to Greece and not have them break my balls

I can not tell them

It s none of their business

After all

It s all their fault

And yet again they ll look at me as if it s mine

Fuck that shit

No wonder they are alone without a daughter

I don't think they are that bad

But why do I think I am

Why

I m not bad for wanting to stay here in London without a daughter just myself

To nurture and to nourish

I need to look after my hair

What shall I do with my hair

I like my hair

Just let it be

Just focus on being an artist

Or a comedian

Or a waitress

Or a moving image

Stick with alex he ll show u how to make a film

Stick to the plan of you as a sensitive person

With a lot of sides

Sex and the city yesterday said they all make up one woman

I said to my boyfriend last nite

Don't break my balls with phonecalls

And don't tell my friends I m dead

I may never pick up

This is how these things are

I ll go upstairs have a hot chocolate and a bath and get on with my life

Fatal error on my computer

Was it a fatal error

I don't like that word

I almost had an accident with the hoover

Are you fuckin stupid

It just reminded me when I almost had an accident in homerton

I don't want to die being nothing

I want to be a famous artist in fact

Fuck it

Why not

They don't get harassed

They are rich

They have the best of both worlds

Or a writer

I mean the ideal possibilities are pretty ideal

You travel

Do ur stuff

Get paid to fly business class

Put it in the expences

And the rest is history

You love good sex

Go do it

Go be like sophie

She s much more intoxicated yet she s filling rooms with people learning about tantric sex

And this is something you believe in

U can be a tantric master

U can be a writer

You can be a copywriter

You can be whatever you want it to be

It being your project

Your project being your life my sweetie

You are the director of this play called your life

Wether u like it or not

You were sent in this planet

With this role

Sometimes fate is a bit different and you die when ur little and born in Africa

But ur you ng and you ng and you are in florida or Miami or London

And you are you and you are here

And now

And here you are

And that is enough of a reason to be happy

You are healthy you can touchtype and you can sort it out

And chances are it doesn't even need sorting out

It just needs the magic cube

The magic portion

You are happy my love and everything around it is just a distraction

Is the salt and pepper that you can do without

Because you are thick and tasty

But in a very strong taste

And a good consistency

And yes

You know it

And whoever meets you for more than five minutes knows it too

Truth is you have fans

You could have a fan club have exhibitions tour the world

I mean you know you can

You also know you are afraid to do it

And you know what

U are right to be afraid

Cos you are fuckin special

And the world is a better place with u in it

And you are quite important

But u feel that u need to help quite desparately

Why not get a water charity

And be an artist that becomes famous organising auctions etc

For water aid

And push that forwards

Creativity

Skills

Charity auctions

Yoga classes

You name it

In the name of art

In the name of life

In the name of thickandtastyxxx

Good work

Good call x

18/11/12

And my life has meaning

It s time to stop

It s time to stop torturing myself

It s time to stop

Give it a go

Time has passed

Time will come by

With me in the same position

Of a drunk taxi driver

Driving a Chevrolet

Masseratti

Jaguar

Happy families

But why do u want to be drunk

Aren't you drunk enough

Haven't u had too much to drink

Too much too soon

Too soon too late

I mean really

Don't you feel sorry for yourself

Will you ever stop

Will you ever stop torturing yourself

You took yourself out of a relationship just as it was starting to work

You coulndn t deal with it

Truth is you still cant

You cant see why you should have another relationship while knowing the end

Truth is you are horny and you want someone like sean to feel free with

Explore his soul and body language

And suck his cock ever after

And you know fair enough go for it

With your baby Israel things weren't that smooth

Do u remember under the bridge

Did we kiss

That s what I m talking about

But there was a certain passion in our relationship that was somehow forced

Into the surface

Truth is Johanna had probably said to her boyf that I was jealous

But yes I was

But I didn't want to admit it

It was a bit like that but also more complicated

Truth is I am complicated

But then again everyone is

Am I self obsessed

I don't know

Is it bad to be

Is it an obsession

Is it not just being interested in who s driving your car

The divine

The upper forces

The outer ego

The you and I and superi and all these

The seventh body

The seventh sense

The sixth sense

The altered states of consciousness

The subconscious

The super conscious

The self development subconscious

Is someone breaking in my house

It s happened before

I m in here I hope not

Distracted

A fly is also flying around the pc

So much fun being a fly in the world

You are so small and it s so big and it s the infinite possibility

And why fly in London

Why not dubai or delhi or thiva

Why else

Why anywhere

My heart goes to hackney wick

I got a change of heart

People need to chase me a little

Just a little

What do u recon

I got to be straight about the whole falling in love thing

Sex is good and yes it comes in layers and tidings

And you know what

Infatuated

So this is what in love is all about

Lust

And that universally accepted weird feeling in ur stomach

What if it s bad cheese

Or lemonade

Anyway thing is I m a bit averse to all this

I stay with the kundalini energy running through my soul and my spine and my seventh body

And you know

Whoever you are thinking of that evokes those baad good times

You are in love right

Wrong

It s lust

But it s strong and it s an extatic experience

Isn't that being in love then

What is it

U got to define love first I guess

Being in love by definition should mean being in the state of love

In love

Is not therefore different to love

Is the way society suggests a failure of marriage

When two people stop being in love

And it means lust

It means when that stomach feeling disappears

And probably sex either starts disappearing as well or becoming good

Meditating and orgasmic

That s what I m talking about

With ian for egsample, I had some good times

I also felt a bit spat out when his girlfriend returned and I had to go

It was all strong experience but on some universal level it felt like life

It was exploring the widths of an emotion

The echos of a dip into action

Isn't that what life is about

X

Love and life is the same thing

You just have to accept it

If you take love out of your life you stop living

You love universally u love yourself and who ever is around you

Ideally

And hate is the reverse so it s a kind of love that is unable to manifest itself

It s a love gone wrong

So eitherway it s love

It s like ice that is melted

But u know the ingredient is there

And trauma

What about trauma

U know it s there as well

It s just a matter of time until it comes to the surface

That s why u have to deal with it

That s why trauma is called trauma

It has the deep resonance and urgency to attend to it

Or at least aknowledge it and consider it

As an omen of something that may come

Like my nipple getting hard

This is a manifestation of a trauma

It s physical and it happens unexpectedly but I do know what that s about

And I do need that rosen method to sort it out

I do

It s a matter of dealing with it

So trauma is a matter to deal with like grey matter

And so long I haven't

Which is obvious

And I should have

And if I had I woulnt feel I should take care of it

And the three years of therapy did a little but not a lot

Not to say I m not in a good place

I m just on some level unrealized

And I m waiting for that to happen

Where really it s about letting go

Taking one thing at a time

And doing things

Just be a doer I suppose

But I m a thinkier

I need a manager

Like the lovely angel I met yesterday

Lovely

Xxxxxxxxxxxxxxxxx

Love my life

Namaste

8.12.12

Its a gun it s a gun its a gun

During times of universal deceit telling the truth becomes a revolutionary act

George Orwell

During times of universal deceit telling the truth becomes a revolutionary act

George Orwell

During times of universal deceit telling the truth becomes a revolutionary act

George Orwell

During times of universal deceit telling the truth becomes a revolutionary act

George Orwell

During times of universal deceit telling the truth becomes a revolutionary act

George Orwell

During times of universal deceit telling the truth becomes a revolutionary act

George Orwell

During times of universal deceit telling the truth becomes a revolutionary act

George Orwell

jeff

Perhaps no one put it better than Thomas Jefferson:

"Those,
which depend on ourselves,
 are the only pleasures a wise man will count on:
 for nothing is ours which another may deprive us of.

Hence the inestimable value of intellectual pleasures.

Ever in our power,
always leading us to something new,
never cloying,
 we ride serene and sublime above the concerns of this mortal world,
 contemplating truth and nature,
 matter and motion,
the laws which bind up their existence,
 and that eternal being who made and bound them up by those laws.

Let this be our employ.

Leave the bustle and the tumult of society to those who have not talents
 to occupy themselves without them."

Kai ti ekana

Fusika kai agxonomai

Den mu aresi o tonos tou kontou kais tin teliki ston idio tono tu apantisa

I mean u know

Kanonika tha eprepe na afxisi to noiki gia ton aprilio

Ah yes

Pernis narkotika agori mu

Exo epireasti ap ti seira pu vlepo

Nomizo oti ime I dalia

Alla imun ligo bitch me ton Israel

Giati

Den katalavaino

Giati me piese

Giati me piezoun olio

Prin kala kala m afisoun isixi theloun na me vgaloun ap to spitaki mu

I mean for the love of god

It s fuckin stressful

It s a beautiful house and I m a beautiful person

And it s not especially safe

And they re Indians and they know it

I ll go to the police and report our door downstairs

It s a little bit broken innit

It s a little bit strange

I don't feel great

I feel like hm dunno a bit apprehensive

Shall I take me out for a coffee in dalston

In homerton?

In the sun?

It s sunny

And snowing

Oh how weird weather

And u know with Israel no I can t be with him he frustrates me to tears

There is no connection

Unfortunately

I do not have a best friend once again and once again I realize how impossible that relationship was

Ok so

What was I saying

I mean really

Fuck it

He – Israel- was gonna give me to my bank account 100 pounds to pay the rent

I mean really

The guy was like oh it s not nothing it s a hundred pounds

Well mister fuckhead

If u consider it s a twelvth of what I ve given u

So if I owed u a fiver I d give u four pounds eighty

And in the end of the day for fucks sake leave me alone

I ve had enough of your shit and you hassling me about the rent like am a criminal

Piss off

What do u want

Ok yes you can rent it to someone else true but don't fuck with me

I m no nobody and I ll bully u back

Cos it is bullying when I m down u push me lower

I mean really

In this situation I m in I cant quite think of a rise in rent

Inflation

Fuck you mister

U didn't even know about stratford

Why dear god am I not into property development

I mean seriously and for real

I can t do it

Fuck s sake

I could look for a cheap property to rent in dalston

And one to buy in fuckforshire

Fuck u mister

U dick

13 3 13

Limited access

so u recon this is how my life is gonna be
limited access
i ll always remember this day- the day i didnt apply for that job
because of the internet connection
do u think there s something not quite right here
do u remind urself too much of that person u trying to get rid of on
the way
chop arms and legs
that person i s you baby
you and ur baby manic responses
rather than throwing a tantrum u kinda say look- i ll check if the
internet is working first please
give me a minute and then i ll order
and this is how you do it
it s ur optimism maybe
whatever it is it s not really paying off- or is it
cos how else would u rite this magic piece
piece of magic
i m hungry and annoyed and iritable and fuckin beahhhh
and this guy yesterday i wanted to tell him to fuck off
i want to sell my staff for thousands of pounds in fact
who cares
no one s gonna buy them anyway
it s a shame i got this online for 250
my career has not started
or has it
it did for a year- then stopped suddenly
as suddely as my encounters with simon
that wasnt suddenly
as fuckin clear as this may be
i dont want to have a commitment
the thing is i dont want to do anything in this life any more
i m hungry
fucks sake
and i m bored of feeling insecure and insufficient
i wanna have a jazmine tea the way ii wanna have it
with the teabag in

and that ladies and gentlemen is my demonstration
and the internet now started working i think
x

lunchbreak

Many years of workplace research has clearly indicated that a failure to take a lunch break reduces personal effectiveness. Controlled studies indicate that assuming a worker arrives to work at 9.00am at 100% effectveness, without a lunch break by 5.00pm they are functioning at less than 35% effectiveness, however is the lunch break is taken the effectivenes at the end of the day is significantly above 50%.

Mai laptop

why do things matter so much
matterial matters

oh that s a good title
or like lick this space
 lick it
i ll just get horny and mastrubate
oh am i allowed to do that
i m kinda
oh dear
i m alone do i feel like every waking up hour is ment to spent with
israel
n
but he understands
he understands and knows and everything
and i love him
i love him dearly
dear oh dear ly
ly dear ly dear
ly is a good name for a dear
dear ly

dearly
derily
deliry
ouuus

but why does he speak german
what is his problem
cos he makes me quite uncomfortable
fuck him
 egsactly that
what about sean
shon
 WHat ABOOUT sheaen
what ABOUT shean

play a soundrack- i love you- always forever- u and me- wishing
together- blabla bla- blablablablabla- bla bla bla- bla bla
bla bla bla- i mean ye- i love my life- all i need to do - is sex
therapy
save us out of breath

Many people

Many people still believe women are just there to be fucked

And if they don't brag about it they actively demonstrate it

By throwing a tantrum dare she say no

Or

Is it just inevitable- in the spur of the moment they are genuinely just frustrated and they start shouting

Thing is I can imagine my mum being in the receiving end of this

Unable to say no she d be just sitting there willing to take it

Unforgiving to herself for being superior she s always curious about female orgasm

And so am I to an extend

I ll be reading lots of books and go to a sex therapist in the end of it all

Hope I don't break up with Israel but truth is I understand it to be a problem

And it s not a small problem as it s the source of every other break up or maybe it s causing it

Thing is if ur not connected at heart level it s kinda unbearable to feel the impact that has on ur sex life= and vice versa

Lets hope things work out for both of us together rather than individually

But i cant help but thinking that we may lose this battle hence each other

And I am really sorry

Me and john

http://en.wikipedia.org/wiki/Frog_%28horse%29

someone called hoof

and me called frog

come together

mm

also ian made me come on and on and what was that effect kundalini sexual energy live

life energy

dear god

I called him baby

I felt like my body was dissolving

Strange kindness from a man

And my pussy was so soft and wet and happy

And he does seem to enjoy it

I mean what is this

How

Does he

How does he feel

He says in the verge of orgasm

But he wont let me touch him too much in case he comes

I did want to lick his dick just lick it once

Ah the thought of it makes me throw my head back and I like that

I like ian

I liked looking at him and

Break-

Looking at his mouth while he was looking for me

And then his little jawline

And his tan

I mean I was in love with the guy

He felt like me

He felt that s what was going on

I didn't kind of expect to feel so much

I remember him saying that he kisses me differently than he kisses other girls

How

I want his tongue

Maybe I don't use my tongue?

No I do! I remember with remy just exploring

19 4 13

Mistreating me

Streaming

How do I allow myself to be so fuckin overwhelmed by a fuckin computer

And why isn't it fuckin changing its letters when I said so

Why

Mm are you happy

Pop my cherries

Told mum and dad

Said it but in my own words

Daddy was really touched and really wanted to go

Really

It broke my heart to say what I had to say

That it was only on for one day the day I was there and then they were gone

Beautiful thing

But it s ok

He was happy

It really was the best I could do wasn't it

I mean under the circumstances

I mean you know what I mean

They are not conservative but I am their daughter

And they would be with me

I mean really

Not really

But I feel bad

He s my dad

And he wanted to be there in the biggest moment of my life

Is like I told them im secretly married

I mean

It s like that

I am sorry

I hope they understand

I hope they do

Cos I don't

I should have told them straight away

I should have

They think it was planned

And I didn't invite them

But it wasn't

They have to believe me

Because of the nature of the film I could not tell them on time

And because of the nature of the performance I couldn't have them watching

I suppose

Still guilt remains

What can u do

I gave them pleasure and they are proud

They can understand

It s massive

It s a massive achievement

Good work girl and as the book said you grow in stages a bit like hops a bit like hopes

Hop hop

Xx

8.6.13

Mmm so frustrating

No fuckin way

Oo oo at least and at last

So yes I officially missed the fuckin deadline

And I feel like shit

But learn ur lesson

U would have felt like shit anyway

U would have found another reason

So yes baby since and u are for the moment a fitness trainer

It would be nice to do a course on computers oh no I mean trainer stuff

So u can get over urself and ur fears

And u know

U do doubt urself so much

Fuck that I m bored of doubting myself and you know I got to start a course in assertiveness

So yes when

M

When I m back

Great

#x

31 1 13

Mmm yoga

So thing is ye

I m not done my yoga yet

As of how I m hanging on

I read this book about man and dog

All I knew is already true

For instance you cant put pressure on ur dog to make u happy

So you cant to ur boyf

You cant rely on either of them to make u feel good about urself

Tricky

Also u have to seem un threatened

Remember for egsample Anastasia

And how u felt quite shit for her being in the same building blah blah

Anyway with Israel relationship was not healthy in so many ways

Aside from kissing

There were too many things wrong in fact

And to be honest I learnt from it

I learnt from that book

I need to make myself feel better

I need more money

I need a career of any sort

But first I need enough money to survive go partying traveling etc

Please it s time you did that now

Look after yourself properly

How

Do some more yoga

Be a bit feisty in how u go about it

And it will come

Don't despair but make ur moves

Play some chess

Do stuff

Do ur yoga

Come on baby I know sometimes we cant get the energy we require

But once we start doing the things that are good for us

As yoga says

We lighten up and we come close to ourselves

Yes

So it s sunny outside u haven't done your yoga what do u recon

U could go for a walk do ur yoga later

Or you could do ur yoga and then go for a walk?

X

16 12 12

My book publishers

http://en.wikipedia.org/wiki/Semiotexte

My fuckin neighbours

the internet and i
ok so massively important- i need some water
wat u gonna do
a rats ass
ah bliss- i love these expressions- what u gonna do- i mean you know-
things and all, getting better and better-
err do you think- err you think- err- dunno. i mean err- for the love
of god- shall i make a cup of tea
 shall i- or shant i - what do u think- violent people people that
scare me fuckin people - i dont need
these people- i mean really is like self punishment. i dont like the
sound of things sometimes. it s bizzare.
i suppose i m a bit apprehensive towards people. what do u want to do-
it s fine but people. people are people.
there are nice people. ignorant people, truthfully refined bohemian
easy going people- these are the ones baby-
nice people. hang out with them a bit more- some people are nice but
particularly boring. cant deal with them.
apart from in social situations- good to hang out with other more
boring people. o h sorry i forgot. or perhaps i didn t/
artificial intelligence. who cares- who gives a shit
people
grigoris is people. remy is people where is remy? i am people. may be
israel is people. may be paul wynter is people?
may be what s his name simon, and jeremy, and richard jerwood- and
miff, and i dunno- charlotte? zax for instance is
people, but will stress me out- a bit full on. antonis is people but
still very inconvenienced in life rather dark.
i dont know why i find myself surrounded by people sometimes that are
not people
ok lets see- toby is people- please keep in touch- mariana and johana
are people but somehow complicated-
neighbours ie ten gales are people but intense rather- butoh marie is
people- the new film makers are people.
boy there s lots of people great
x siraz is people-
see you people

New everything

I m pretty much immobilised

Financially paralysed

I had a thought about the dosh and even so I m fucked or am i

Yes I am

I mean fuck

I just realized

Fuck

I ll have to check

I was gonna talk about men

I texted my dad

I don't like it

They force it upon me when they say they love me that I should love them too

I don't know what love is

It s complicated

Lets say I text it back out of politeness

In any case I was gonna talk about men

And how after the book I m able to understand them

Yes

That s something I realized when aged ten the bad boy of the school started hunting me down

After my mum s advice that I should play hard to get

up until that point I had just hunted him down I suppose

and then boom

the closest we ever got

I was laying down and he was laying on top of me

By the toilets

Ooh that s as good as it gets

I don't know but I do remember being in the balcony of my house deciding that it wasn't my victory

I wasn't gonna play by their rules and when I did and won I didn't enjoy it

So same again years later with my boyfriend at the time

I remember I read that article that said tell ur man blah blah don't you think so or it was your idea or sthing

And they ll instantly agree and do it

So I remember distinctly copying a phrase and getting that reaction and feeling instantly disappointed

Oh well

I m doing it again soon

Every seven years -more like every ten years

So yes it s good it may work it may well work

I need to pass on the knowledge to elefteria and then I ll have succeeded as a godmother

Lets see

And then

Be a comedian a famous artist and a writer

11 1 13

New Text Document

so ye- that was annoying and made me shake- you dick.

Nice tip

"If you wish to achieve worthwhile things in your personal and career life, you must become a worthwhile person in your own self-development."

No but

no but that s irrelevant
i m now realizing i had a better impression of elisa after she met roger-
and then i felt immediately threatened when she met israel
i mean i dont even want them in the same sentence
i ll just block my window from the world=
a bit rude but come on ur allowed to protect ur own property
my space
and yes i know it s wrong but it feels wrong and kinda undoable
interestingly i ve done worse i m sure
i ve lost touch with my mum for god s sake
u with me

No I mean

Congratulations. She congratulates him on doing a good kus kus. Bloody Chinese you may well die, just imagine the whole of china, empty. Joy

No this is terrible, fantasies are terrible, and then oops a big rock hit the last one! Tvouz

Cartoon character, eyes on floor. Going straight. Get me. I never have come across a Japanese person I did not like.

Now I like Chinese food I guess but that doesn't say anything

We can still have british Chinese .

Like madagaskar,,,,

Like champagne and strawberries

Like tiramisu

And why black people have not heard of it

Why

I d lick his ass I ve had passionate sex with two black people

I m not a racist

Hm old argument#]

Anyhoo

What about simon

What about simon

What about simon

What about what about writing or just blathering

Writing for myself or writing for the world I cant decide

It doesn't work

It really really doesn't

I don't like it when I write to make sense

I don't want to make sense

Sensei

This is for me therefore

All four

I ll beat you up

I m sure he had a fantasie about his prescious little flatmate

Maybe that s why I don't like her

I don't like her

I just don't

I don't

Fuckin don't then

Ok then

We re done

What my therapist was saying was if you don't like someone don't pretend you do

What yoga is saying is that when u don't like someone is actually a very physical thing

And I agree

It s physical

Veery physical

Like I could burn you down and see the flames

What if she s innocent

Innocent?

Why doubt me

Didn't she say that oh u have a girlfriend it s not fair

Didn't she

If she asks me how long are you guys going out

What do I say

What do I say

How long about a year and a bit I think

Or what would be the right answer for you to fuck off

If I won the lottery I d tell you to fuck off

Fuck off

I can tell you now

Innint

I just did

It s not nice to have a bad relationship with my boyfriends flatmate but hey what do u do

I mean

Dunno

What can you do o

What can you do o

What can you do o

O o

O a

Oi filoi mas len

Enen

Xxxxxxxxxxxxxxxxxxxxxxxxxxxxxxxxxxxxxxxxxxxxxxxxxxxxxxxxxxxxxxx
xxxxxxxxxxxxxxxxxxxxxxxxxxxxxxxxxxxxxxxxxxxxxxxxxxxxxxxxxxxxxxx
xxxxxxxxxxxxxxxxxxxxxxxxxxxxxxxxxxxxxxxxxxxxxxxxxxxxxxxxxxxxxxx
xxxxxxxxxxxxxxxxxxxxxxxxxxxxxxx

It s a gun

Yes it s a gun in my pocket I m not happy to see you

Xxxxxxxxxxxxx

It s a good line no? no? innocently

Tvvoouu

Ahha this is fun

A Chinese girl popped through my advertisments on my laptop and she says she wants a professional looking cv

How about a professional looking scar

Scarface

Another girl needs a calendar to keep up with everything

Ooo this is fun

Who are these people on my desktop and what do they want

Who cares

Xxxxxxxxxxxxxxxxxxxx

What can you do o.....

I m happy bout today I got stuff to do that reinforce reincarnate and rein my thinking

I do think I will show this

But I don't want to

I don't want to think like this this is boring I don't like it

I like the happy to see me joke tho

Tvou

It s a classic

A classic joke

A classic

I mean classic

Hahahahahahaaaaaahaaaaaa oh no

No

No

No

Nooo

I mean noooooo

It s like nooooooooooooo

Noooooooooooooo

Noooooooooo

5/10/12

No real what

No real willingness to succeed

Ah as I d never be happy

As happy wasn't objective

Wasn't the objective

The aim

What was it

U don't try to slack u just work hard

Like a Chinese

And then die

Like a Lebanese

Of poverty

Like I m hungry now

Like I haven't eaten properly today

Thank god for the porridge

And you know

I could have had

I might have done

I mean what is it

What

Who

M

Boy George was saying I m more like me

And me too

I m more like me am i

Or I m so far ahead I can see myself coming

I m me in ians arms as well

I am still me

I don't get lost in him or in anyone

I m me and I m full of myself

It s good

It s that definition I would never work out

As I know there are no boundaries it s all energy and atoms and we all blend together

That s why being a racist doesn't exist

It s just a colour u don't want to be associated with

Thing is it s a bit like that

U see it

It s there

But if you magnify it and analyse it its just fresh air

Isn't that beautiful

All these clouds around us making masses etc

Deadly sometimes

Thick dense nothingness over people

Products over people

A horse over people

And beyond

Beyonce is made of nothing

But we knew that

What about Madonna

She seems content and intact

But she s also bubbles

A hell of a lot of bubbles

Like carrie bradsaw

Yes is that her real name

What about

Me

I m made of bubbles too

And cherries

And I ll be popping them for the rest of my life

Celavie

Fucks ssake

x

Noo o

nothing new
internet s not working again
it seems that this is where my problems start
internet looking for jobs made impossible
getting money made imposs
self esteem down the drain
or at least a glimse of it as i earn some fifty quid here and there
new level of stress looking at the possibility of the housing situation
arising in the horizon
arise- horize- horisontan
dental
floss
da
x

Nothing ever prepares me

Baba se parakalo min kukloforis me to vraki su m enoxli

Might have done

Could have said

As Samantha puts it, men are like monkeys

They want to show it off

True

Samantha is what got me by in my darkest hours

I suppose it s something I have the choice to confront

Or to live with

Yes it bothers me

My dad was waiting for me to return his mobile half with his pants down

I mean why

What is there to see and why such hard work

And what goes through your head is the worse

I feel sorry for me and him

He thought of it

And I was surprised

Now about my thoughts and feelings

I feel hurt and sorry

And confused and angry and scared

Scared of what it may do to me

As a situation

What it may trigger what fuckin thougts and anger from the past transferred into the future

I don't want to fuck my future

Or my present

Or my presence

I want to be a true yogi with positive thoughts and forgiveness

Nothing but forgiveness

Can you forgive the monkey in your living room

I suppose

If I see it for what it is

A monkey

Someone that turns into a monkey

Can I be prepared for the switch

Can I tell the monkey off

I mean I don't know I could as I said

Yes I should be true to myself and say please dad make sure u don't get changed in front of me cos I feel uncomfortable

I could well do that in a nice way and without creating any weirdness

Yes I could

I so could

May be I ll go to the lengths of actually doing it

I mean why not

I deserve to clear the air for him and for me

He may look at me as if I m fuckin mad

But I m not but I may well be

That s the scary part

I feel at some point I ll go nuts

Like proper nuts

With the certificate and everything

And I hate doctors and white rooms and shit

But that s where I see me in those events

Or shooting heroin that s another outlet

I mean I don't like self harm as a solution

It does seem to come handy though instead of having an assertive semi uncomfortable conversation

Why honey

Ok they are your parents but hey

The other thing

Mum said she don't hate anyone

But why

Why not hate the guy that sexually abused me as a child

Why hate someone else instead

Why not hate the right fuckin guy

I m struggling with forgiveness amongst my family

But I am doing yoga

And I m reading yoga

And I try to eliminate the angry samskaras

And the negative ones

And create new ones instead

And deal with conflict

I d like to do a weekly based assertiveness course

It really suited me

It made me feel good about my life made me ask for things and put things straight

Even with my mum it helped

Ok I broke up with my boyfriend but the truth is I was having a rough time during the end wasn't i

I probably was n t assertive enough= it was in the beginning and I coulnd t quite communicate how deeply uncomfortable I felt with his extra whore flatmate

The sweet thing

I m not sure about any of it anymore

It may have been the hormones

May be the hormones

It s always the hormones

The truth is I was on a sort of pill

And yes I was up and down and sideways and I came twice during sex which has never happened before

And another thing

We broke up

Just on our peak of my sexual satisfaction the day after we broke up

Broke up into tears

If

Still

Yet

All these

Bloody fuckin petrol station

Whatever the fuck it was

I don't know

His jaw dropped

And is it or is it my mum s fault

It was a weird time

But

I went skiing

And I met simon

And I met john to alogaki

I like john to alogaki and I have a task for when I go home

Ride it

Ride it hard and feel the rhythm

I love the guy

I love the way he made me laugh and made me blush and made me come

And I mean the guy

The guy

Is a genius

A form of genious

He s beautiful

He is handsome

He is like a freakin hippy of a hippodrome

He is the dog s bollox

He s the dog

The top dog

He s a horse

He s a horse

Ah

X

A moment of silence

I do admire horses

I admire a horse for it s beauty and capacity to captivate you and thrill you and overcome you with thunder

And almond oil

A horse is sheer power and beauty and the rhythm of life

And he does this thing with his lips

I mean the guy

The guy is a horse and he s just for me

But

As yoga has it

Ok I wont claim him

I ll leave him out there to be shared

I mean he is a horse and you have to give him that much

The chance to ride

Run wild

I don't want to tame him

I don't need to

I just need a ride

A fuckin ride

Like a junkie needs a hit

It s a story

I didn't need a ride that bad with a man or with a horse before

Or did i

May be with tim

Yes I remember being on tim s floor looking at him begging to let me suck his cock

This was not verbally expressed by no means but I do remember the feeling

I remember looking at him and I still remember how he looked and why the crush

This one now

It s a new crush

A whole new crush

With a horse with a personality of a horse as well

The guy is not helping

I m quite unnerved

I don't know

I mean come on

Please

I d like to be with him and make me come and make him scream

What would he do just yawn

I want to see the world with him

But I think of simon

Either

Really

I want to see the world through an orgasmic delight

Afternoon delight

I have seen the world like this

I have been with ian and tim and had fun

And a couple of times with Israel

And could be nice to know that I ll just go along alongside a horse

Ride with it or kinda run attached to it

I don't know

I mean I like him I love him and I d like to suck him suck a horse

I mean eitherway

It doesn't matter I d like him to choke me gently and have a bit of sean

Be nice

X

22 2 13

O k so

There is a certain risk in the life I m living

Is t liver disease

Or chromosome incapacity

Or maladjustment

Or malnutrition

It s that mainly

It s the fact that no one not even me understands how broke I am

And I often try to neglect the fact that I m broken

But I mean I m getting to know me as we said

He spoke to me like I intended that

It was a fuckin accident

People die in accidents

You can be angry with me for making a mistake and causing an accident

But the truth is I am angry with yourself for lending me your favourite projector

And I am angry with myself for accepting it

I am also angry that although I considered it to be heavily heavy I still took it

I am angry I said to emma I have a projector when I clearly didn't

I am angry with the fact that I was going to bring a projector from London here and why

Why

I mean I really shouldn't

I should just say I fuckin hate to shit carrying stuff

And I m going to bricklane tomorrow first thing in the morning guess what carrying stuff

I am angry at the way I feel right now

And that I m so upset

I got upset because he got angry with me and he told me off about something and that he s right

I mean look at it

I don't especially like carrying stuff

Which is why I shouldn't

In so many ways

I mean really

What can I say

Maybe try to sell the paintings?

Maybe try to just go home early

Maybe pretend this day never happened

But it did

And it s still here

And I have in theory time to change it

But I m just really upset

I keep crying

And I can t find the strength or I haven't got the will to change it

Or I m too proud and ashamed of myself

And I feel like a little child

And even with Israel I feel that in a way with him I had a fight as well

Troleyology

Maybe contact them

May be try live your life to the full

May be just try

Maybe you can take it back

Maybe you are just upset and embarrassed

Maybe you can just stop and take it from here

From the top

Re set

Maybe this is what this day is about

Sometimes you just have to say

I m sorry

I didn't mean to drop the fuckin thing

I hoped it was all right

Now I know it s not

I still hope it was all right

Now I know not to borrow shit

Now I know why I do not like to borrow shit

It s just you know I got carried away

To be honest

I did and I can t take it back

I can only take it from the top

I am more upset that someone offered to show my film with a different projector and I said no

I m sorry I said no

I didn't mean to say no

I just didn't react properly

I was upset and getting a panic attack

I said no where I should have said yes

I should have said I m really upset right now

I m really upset right now

I m really upset right now

I m really upset right now

I m really upset right now

I m really upset right now

I m really upset right now

I m really upset right now

I m really upset right now

I m really upset right now

I m really upset right now

I m really upset right now

I m really upset right now

I m really upset right now

I m really upset right now

I m really upset right now

I m really upset right now

I m really upset right now

I m really upset right now

I m really upset right now

I m really upset right now

I m really upset right now

I m really upset right now

I m really upset right now

I m really upset right now

I m really upset right now

I m really upset right now

I m really upset right now

I m really upset right now

I m really upset right now

I m really upset right now

I m really upset right now

I m really upset right now

I m really upset right now

I m really upset still

Still really upset

Right now

Right now

I m just you know pretending I m ok

But the truth is I m really upset right now

Right now

Right now

Now

I m angry

I m better

I m only better and I was only angry at the coffee machine sound

I mean really why are they allowed

Why are we here to relax yet we are getting abused

I want to go to venice and stay there

I like venice

It s much quieter and nicer and it s simple and you know I get it

Where here It s abusive and I have to live through it and I know it but no one else seems to know it

Why ask me now

I m really upset right now

I m really upset right now

I m really upset right now

Am a bit better right now

Ok I made a mistake the first one was an accident

Then I should have tried to play it

But then I wouldn't borrow it again

So on the plus side I d be In London – less upset I guess but I had a nice time on my train here and it was seven pounds

Not too bad

I ll do that again

I mean

It s nice being by the seaside just remember how bad can it be?

It s not that I leave things to the last minute cos I don't

It s cos you know it s all a bit up in the air and I want to keep going but I need to work as a result or direct consequence or prerequisite

However you look at it

I pissed popadom off

Yes I understand I should have told him before

I should have

Ok so then he should have not given me his fave projector

It was sweet of him

I should have said no

I should have

I wish I had said no

I mean really

Who gives a fuck I mean in the end of the day I should have said can I have one that s not your favourite

I mean I kinda suggested that I d break the lense

I m a little telepathic whichever way you look at it

I just didn't want to take that fuckin massive lense

And can u blame me for that sesriously?

Who s gonna blame anyone for anything

I feel like shit and I feel cold and miserable

And I do feel I have learnt today

I don't borrow someone s favourite equipment

I don't lend someone my favourite thing in life

I don't generally carry heavy shit cos I fuckin hate it and the action upsets me and I feel really miserable

I eat well and if I haven't got money I get a fuckin flatmate

I try to be sensible about life and treat it with respect

I balance myself through yoga or writing

I keep up with my art therapy once a day

All these things went wrong before anything went wrong with the projector

That s why I m upset

And that s why I m fuckin crying#

Yeah

Cry I t s good for you

But remember to do the stuff from above

I m glad u r a dancer and you do your tten min dance a day in the morning

It s good for the soul

It s certainly waken urs up and have made u who you really are since 35 th bday

Good on you

You are a good therapist to yourself

And possibly to other people

You are pretty fuckin cool trainer as well

And you like to do your job correctly

And if anything you are trying enough

And now you ll be doing a course for which your employer pays yeyy

And you ll be even better that before

And you ll get more hours with ceryl

And generally you ll be fine

And you are

You ll just be lets say on the bright side

And you ll have time for pizza

And time to pay for it

And you wont have to eat it on ur own in front of the tv

You are upset because u are making yourself miserable

Because your dad told you years ago that you don't know how to live

And the truth is you think you don't

You do but it really needs to be addressed

You are sensitive

And you need good food and rest and quietness

And this London for you at the moment is hectic

That s it

It s too much for anyone

Let alone you

You are gambling in the seat of madness

And you know it

Which is good

You don't crack under pressure cos u think it s cool but it d be easier if you did

I don't wish u did but the combination of the two puts u in a vulnerable position

Your limits are lax and you are borderline with the absolut chaos

But u are on top of it

But that takes all the effort in the world

Being in this café is plain abuse mate

The fuckin caffe maschine

I mean seriously cant we just sue them

I think I would like to come up with a maschine to keep the caffe mashines quiet

I t s quality of life and it caters for a better future, less tinnitus and more relaxing cafes staff and customers

I m gonna have to look into it

And what about the emptiness of the coffee

We can perhaps scoop it with a spoon

Yes may be that as well

It could be an idea

And then the filter

The sound parrier

The filter that stops the sound pollution

I could work with dyson or with siemens or make a greek company even better

That produces coffe machine quitet filters

That would be nice

And charge them at a hundred pounds a pop

Mm nice

Better already

Cos I mean it s the till and the spoons and the change

And I guess all these could be avoided if there was a kind of bubble air system to prevent sound from travelling

Ah nice and quiet moment

She s getting a cappuccino! I knew it

Oh well I suppose…

Ok ime

Ime eroteumeni me to moro mu

Isn t it great

Den ime eroteumeni me to moro tis allis

As poume

I don't know

U know

It s a bit bizzare, when ur friend is not your friend etc etc- it s a bit like hm- what do u recon

Are you happy

Blazing happy

Blazing superstar happy

I mean

U can give up a friend for a doubt, a bad feeling a disbelief etc etc

U can decide u feel threatened by someone and give them up

Innit

I do think that actually, fair enough it could happen both ways

I mean fair enough

It s kinda like hm dunno

A bit bizzare

People don't expect it from me they don't see it coming

They don't expect me to be insecure

Ok and why – I just also feel that at some level idiosyncratically I don't work like that

I mean yes god damn im a mad

Like whorehopping= whaat???

I say shit god damn I m a man!!!!!! Should be fun

We get better orgasms-if and when we do

Do we yes we do I shay shit goddam im a man

Love my life and love my boyfriend

And I m happy

Good be happy

I say shit god dam im a man

No bt I m very much a woman

Ok so so

It seems to me that my therapist is pissed off with me and with him/

It s a tricky one

And me too for that countertransference

Who gives a fuck

I finally do

I actually do

I do give a fuck about me

That s good

And if that s how I feel= which I suspect it is

I am going to act on it

If he feels different

Let me know=- he will

But- in the end of the day, I need to do a few things on my own

Someone allocated me a therapist from the nhs a long time ago

And someone diagnosed me as depressed

A long time ago

And yes who gives a fuck= again and again

I think I need to make songs so it ll be like

Give me the tune I ll write you a song

What do u want it to be about

The tune?

The story of my life

Happy beatles

Happy families

Ok so the film

The film is gonna be like this

Anything and everything goes

The plot at the back is the story at the back of a dvd

I shall document more things such as my love life at the mo

Say a bit about orgasmic meditation

Look into it

Experiment with life

Life is an experiment

An experience

Make it fun

Make it last

Make it yours

I remember when tom – a rapist- told me how he felt about cheese

No I m just thrown a bit

Oh yes when he told me about tim that I respect him too much

When I do that I suppose I m in awe

I don't feel I want to play any more its more of a passive ahh

Do u remember when dan came in the room

I remember distinctly I wouldn't speak I would just sit there

And when I went for a drink with dan and tim I think in all accounts it was my dream team

But I was so into tim at that point, I was full with desire , explosive and exploring sex and inhibitions and falling in love and falling asleep in an expensive mattress

These were the days

I was incapable of forgiveness that s not ture

I had to forgive too much

But on the bright side sex was slow and tim was a great kisser

I mean he still is

I mean you know

You know what I mean

You know

In all accounts I feel I ve had a good life before I start looking into it

I never took a moment to stop and think what is it that makes me so unhappy

It s that feeling of mates a group of people something that Israel is doing at the moment

I guess I m kind of doing it too in some ways

Yes kind of

But not so much

Say camila can be a good friend, elisa is, zoe is but she s busy, remy is waking up to the fact I need him, now if I brought these people together more often

Maxa is fun

Sabine is fun

Niki is a bit hard to get

I m still not challenged

I want russel brand and brad pitt in my living room

So simon

Remy

Adam

Tina of girls

Hege

Camila

So this is the question

Who would you stay stuck on the lift with

Mmm

Israel no

Remy yes I would laugh

Zeco I would start fucking him

Charlie is pretty cool

Mungo if he wasn't a wanker

Shall I contact them again

Shall i

Shall I just start behaving normally towards my old friends and towards my life??

Ok yes time to let go

To new beginnings

And new ends

X

No ends

29/10/12

Ok so what have we got

What was the connection with my family

They did let me down

And I did let them down

So I feel that I m doing the same with society

If I stop letting myself down with society do u think I ll stop letting my parents down

Do u think If I stop for a second just stop stop

Just stop

What s it gonna be

The here and now

How long

How many years of therapy

How bizzare

I just cant do it any more

I feel sick actually

I feel this tremendous wave of sickness running over me

I feel I may be pregnant

In which case things will be different

And all together much more

But still

What the fuck

Am I supposed to take anything on or nothing at all or what

What is it that u want my little pumkin

I love you

So

Yes I keep letting them down and society down

But

I d let my parents down anyway wouldn't i

Like my dad made a joke about my graduation

He would always find something to say

I mean really

That s it

There never seems to be a point in trying as I m gonna feel like I let them down anyway

So I may as well do it from the beginning and do it well and fuck it downright

I wanna die and I wanna live

I think I ll sue housing benefit

Yes I will

Yes I will.

So this three months have been about housing benefits

Yes I mean really

It s been emotional

I cant be having such a bad time over something

It could be cancer

It kinda should be

I either should not take it that seriously

Or I shouldn't internalise it

Actually I cant believe nothing is sorted

Ok so

Dunno what do u recon

People break up all the time and all the time I feel like I m gonna break up

Thing is with people I don't really care about sex usually works

Say with simon it was just he was old there wasn t a threat of commitment of some sort or boyfriendhood

With tim I didn't wanna do it cos I hadn't enjoyed sex by that point

But I did cos I was melting while I looked at him

But we did spent all day in bed pretty much watching films hangin out the energy was building it was like foreplay

With Israel my foreplay time is limited and the cock starts trying to get into my pussy

He s not teasing me

He does it in real life maybe I should tell him that

He should do it in bed

But that requires thinking and he doesn't want to think

Ok

It s like a trivial like a puzzle

I don't think it s gonna work

I m trying to prepare myself for the possibility

I ll be crying for months whereas he ll be fine

Typical really

He ll be out having fun shagging people maybe or may be not

But that aint the point as he wont be shagging me

Dear old me

No one will be shagging me

Im scared that he ll dump me and

Why dear god is it so scary

Fucks sake I don't care

I ll find a roomshare somewhere I ll start renting with people again I just need a big room

And yes my art can go somewhere like I don't know

A bin or a trash place

It doesn't really matter does it

I mean what s with anything these days

It ll be better to find a house and find the flatmates for once

And maybe use my connection near crouch end to find something in hackney

Why not

See how it goes really

And maybe I can keep a second room to be my studio

I love my life already

Xx I embrace change and chance

And I wont hang from israels balls that s for sure

And I can tell him what I like and what I don't

I don't like feeling passive and used

I ve had that role for most of my adolescence when I thought sex was a bunch of shit

Now I now I can enjoy it but I also know that

A it s a selfish act

B it s a we task

And while we r at it I need to be super relaxed like I m meditating

And you need to be available for teasing and pleasing

And yes we may fuck eventually in the end or I may wank you off

But the bottom line is I want to be there and I want to feel involved

And if I don't I ll be gone next time

Nanait

Just remembered the disaster time with this guy simon

I said to him something and he didn't do it

And I got up wore my clothes

Then he became a bit better again

Then the same happened

Wore my clothes

Left

Stood on kingsland road and felt a bit better

Fresh air rain but hey a sense of freedom

I think on some level I want to challenge the neediness I feel in regards to Israel

It s almost like hm I cant contain myself

Which I cant anyway

And I feel like I m a bit scared of my surroundings

So ye

I could get a different boyfriend

I could have some fun couldn't I ??

Why do I want to be with Israel again

He s what

He s over?

He s sweet

He cant

He chooses not to

Dunno

He wants to play kinky and he s sexually blocked up

He s tight and he s got a tight back

To be honest I feel connected to him but as they say

There s something I don't like about me- in him

I don't know

We got similar sex issues

We could talk about them

I could explain to him that I like his cock soft

And I like the idea of playing around in sex

And I want to feel part of it

I want to enjoy it

Remember alex

I was horny and in love and I was getting dumped

How horrid

And then he said all I m gonna do I ll do this and this and that

And he did

And it was great

I like my pussy being wet it is accommodating

I like my pussy munching away knowingly

I loved sex with simon

Yes I have glorified it

But it was good

I mean I d travel that far

I hope Israel doesn't fuck anyone

Then again that s all I want?

No

I want human interaction

I want him to be playful in bed and allow me to be

I don't want the fear of the penetration hangin over my head

I mean really what is that

Am I supposed to relax

Is it like ooh I got it hard got to stick it in

It really isn't working glad we talked about it

Im not looking forward to another confrontational moment

I m not looking forward to seeing him in so many ways

I m actually really upset with me

I cant be that sorted person but thing is I can get orgasms with other people

Correct

What was that buy a tempur mat

Yes love

go

Ok still

So

He said

And I said

And he said

And it s all kinda in the air

One thing I read today

Everything I have done in my life so far have led me to this moment right now

I like it

It s a pretty good moment

I wish I don't split up with my boyfriend

I wish it s all a passing phase of exploring exploiting and exercising

The possibilities are endless

And this is somehow new knowledge

Is like a whole new book to a whole new chapter called my life

How funny

And it s about acceptance

And hiv positive

It s not funny any more

Life is not funny

Or is it

It s all a bit like hm dunno imimathia

Half learning

Better than non learning

What about what about Britney and kissing workshops and intimacy and fuckin tequila sunrise

What about sunset in santorini and clapping with the Chinese tourists

Fuckin Chinese

No I like French

Baquette and kissing

What about paris

What about just rambling on and on like a peasant on crack cocaine

What about dalston and the mews

What about haggerston and indo and all these beautiful people

What about andy Warhol

What about meeting people doing a sculpture course

What about

Me

Me in all this

Swimming in the pool of possibilities

Ducking the leaves

Pool is green shiny from the sky

Life is beautiful

And I ve just had a beautiful orgasm with a beautiful guy in a well lit room

All very cinematographical

A strangely seductive setup where you jump with both feet

What do u do

Life is beautiful

And sometimes u just have to live it

For what it is

For what its worth

What do u do

It is seductive

And it s a nice surprise after a nutella chocolate

And a poetry worksop

Boom

Back into tescos

U bump into the guy

The guy you were thinking of phoning

And you take it from there

Do chicken know that everything tastes like chicken

Not everything tastes like chicken

Beautiful chicken

I loved myself today

And my breasts

And my pussy

And everything about me

I loved being responsive and happy and lively and alive

And you know

Quite positively

Making a choice

Making a statement and after all

Life is beautiful

And my barbies keep smiling

Ce lavie x

Good fuck in French

11/11/12

orgasm

So

As it happens

When it happens it apparently doesn't mean anything

Or so they say

Or so it seems

Or they don't know

Or whatever

But

When it doesn't happen

It ruins everything

So when it happens It doesn't fix anything

And when it doesn't happen it ruins everything

What is it

An orgasm!

Questions

In a relationship:

Haha

Oh well

Parapente text

Ine ligo ponokefalos to parapente ligo vavoura

Ine kai loipa kai loipa

Tora as pume ftiaxno to tsagaki mu kai tha to pio kai tha kano tin texni mu kai meta tha pao pros tas performance

I mean u know

Elpizo na min me xexasi o allos

Den to xexase apla u know

In any case

It s up to u

Up to me

Up to all of us

I love the fact that I m stretching more with a deadline ☺

I said every hour good idea

I m doing it now

23 3 13

Pes mu

Ime kourasmeni thelo na kimitho

Where is dick

Where

Where

I love dick

X

I am polyamoruous

But yoga says I m not

So how much egsactly do people want to pay for rent

And what were they thinking

I mean 130 pounds a week is a lot but we re in London and it s a nice flat

Innit

And I mean I really don't like his girlfriend and I really feel that she could be a threat

And I don't like him

It s a bit like hm I don't like to live with you in that energy

It s like hell in my opinion

He s tense and horrible and dark and he s been in the army

I mean why the hell do I want to live with him

And he fancies me and I don't trust him

So no is the answer

Sorry

Maybe I should tell him

No today

Innit

x

Plan be

- i also write stuff and am an artist as well, i want to know how to publish something and how to make it for sale as in your link- the basket purchase thing, i also teach yoga and i want something like that for a yoga class ie a purchase thing- i guess they are all very different, my main question was how to publish my writings/ print them, and have them available for sale - and then how to advertise them. auta

-
00:37
Anthony Anaxagorou

Ok. I'll be honest it's very hard selling you work if people aren't familiar with your material. The main problem I found when I started self-publishing in 2009 was that the only people who would buy my books would be family and friends. To really broaden your reader-base you will need to utilize both YouTube, social networks as well as live performances. You can set up an e-shop using Big Cartel to sell your products via a website but besides that it's still pretty difficult getting people to part with money, especially if it's something they haven't read or seen performed before.

-
00:40
Maria Tsartsali

mm interesting stuff- i think i should make a switch to some sort of stand up career now that i m still young- ish, and then carry the book with me. got a plan, thank you! still coffee if you like.

Pple I said no to

James Putnam

Mr serotta

psychanalisis

Very true too true, yes. And so . therefore. What would you like to say, what about, fuck that was heavy what about this justice what about Justin Hoffman what a bout what about,,, cheezy films, networking, teleporting, telesporting, lovelyhood , I mean, is it all about treating each other well.

And what does it mean

And why

Are you mean

You men

I can t generalize it

So my dad lets have it written

He again touched my chest with the back of his arm as soon as I got here

And when we had dinner he was looking at the mirror behind me

And yes he is acting upon it

And then he I saw him changing again.

Ok it s just that he s acting upon it

That s what the therapist says

Feelings are feelings is when u act upon them

Ok

But

Let s have it

I mean there is no reason to have no physical contact

But it has to be non perversive

And that s it

How do u do that

U do lots and lots and lots of yoga

And then I don't know pray meditate go to the beach

It s all part of a universal plan

It s what it is

U can put up some sort of comments

You can discuss things you don't like

State them simply

Say sthin like be careful of my chest as it is sore

Why are you looking at the mirror? I guess it can be anything ,

Are you looking at the back of my neck

Are you

Are you my father and you are letting me down

In a massive way

But then again what matters is that yes I keep it together and why would I collapse with the weight of someone else

Letting me down

No one can actually let me down

No one can let me up or down

I am mee

I am floating

And yes on occasion I build some castles made of sand and the people step on them with their bare feet

But that s about it

They ruin my impression of them

They shatter my world

But not me

Cos I m mee I m not in it

I am a spirit without a doubt and I pass fleetingly through the castles

My body makes them

My physical body

And their physical body steps upon them

But my spirit is high

My mind is trying to catch up make sense keep it together

But what

Is it gonna go

Take a leap

Take a holiday

Have a nervous breakdown

It s my physical body that has a reaction towards wha their physical body does

But my spirit will swiftly pass by ask my physical body for assistance and allowance to help put some effort to keep up with the pressure the physical pressure

So do some yoga

And my mind- will rest, monitoring, making sense, working it all out, kind of saddened and confused

Sand ,, like the sand sad and confused

Lets see if we can change anything

We can definitely stay within and change our reaction

Our world

A fuckin documentary on anger

A praise to yoga

A praise to me, and me again,.

19/8/12 midnite- but not, ten fifty in greek time

I mean he s struggling

He knows there s something wrong

He knows and he tries to fish it out

Do I reject him

Do I think he s a pervert

Do I think he s out of order

He asks

Yes these are my thoughts

He s suffering

Because of me= not

Because of something else

Because of him I guess

Because of life

Because he doesn't know

How he let me down and failed to protect me

And now he s being a pervert

It s not easy being me I swear

But then again who knows

No one knows anything about anyone

It s not easy being anyone I suppose

And I suppose I m right

Do some yoga

I mean it

Do something help yourself sort it out

Treat yourself

Don't waste it

It s an opportunity to stand by yourself with what you got and be free

No reason to suffer

Whatever it is

You are made of you

You are you babes

You are you your unique material your printed imprint your blue cool imprint

And yes it s hart I get it

I really do

And I ll stand by you and I ll be with me and I ll try not to split

I ll be united and I ll be within

I ll be without no

I ll be free to travel to go to unravel

Interpret loose lose oh gone

Am scared

I get it

I m scared I cant take it any more

My body Is weak, my physical body is weak and my physique is weak

And there is no but

You hadn t seen you r dad for a long time

Make this time different

Make an effort to express yourself in a way that makes sense

If you wish

Or just write

I mean you can say that I am a woman and you are a man and you are my dad but what you see is a woman that is your daughter

Because this is the truth

I mean if my dog turned out to be a big dog I would still see a big dog that was still my dog

I mean you can t see a small dog as there is n t in the room

I am a woman and I feel quite uncomfortable around naked pictures in the house I mean it s all a bit too erotic

I am at home and to be honest it s ok to keep the erotic pictues in the bedroom and if you both agree

You need a woman to paint I mean

I know you disapprove of efi saying about sex and yet she s right and it s all worked out for her in her sexual life am afraid

Not in yours I m afraid

And I know that as all this oppression and frustration comes to me

And I m sorry

I am not causing it so I keep saying but the truth is I feel like you should have been in a tantric course with mum

You should be fuckin other women and let it out of your system

And not your daughter

And not perve on cats

I mean I m sorry but I am just present in someone s frustration

I m like an outlet ston evgatsi tis gitonias

But that s my dad

And he s rather suttle

But not too suttle for me as nothing is

So yes

I understand

I get it

And why should it bring me down

Of course he s my dad and of course he s suffering

Of course I get it

Of course I m sorry for him

But also for me as I m here swimming in a house of frustration

Is my house like that

It s kinda trying to get rid of it my house is

Oh dear god

All these years of frustration take another three times the years to get out of it

Isn't it

And its maths

It s all maths

Its all there ever is

And the spirit

Thirty per cent]

read

A woman

A very interesting theory

Tear there

Second one:

Detach

I ve come a long way

Twin sista- is it trying

Would you say- the one with the shit

!! aand the winner is

Right then

Every day is a new day

And you have to treat it like that

Not like a continuation of the old day

An old day

Any old day

And time to reflect is a bit like a waste of time

Or not

I mean today I woke up with my boyf we went out to the park he was feeling a bit shit

And so was I to one level

I had have to endure the flatmate once again

It was a difficult morning

I mean the girl wont shut up talkin shit out of her ass

I mean really

Now maybe she apologises

I think she should

I mean really

What was that about

He is only nice to you

She finds me in times when I m happy and tired

Anyway I mean

Then we played chess

It wasn't relaxing

I m sorry

I can t relax over there at the moment

I ll have to talk to her

Yes I will

I ll say I feel that I need to talk to u about something

When we first met Israel was cookin dinner and I heard you sayin it s not fair you got a girlfriend it s not fair

I feel I need to know why u said that

What do u mean

Oh I didn't say that

And if I did I said it as a joke

Because he can cook

And I wish I get a boyfriend that can cook

Ok good

I wish you do too

If that s what you want

But at the same time you know I felt a bit hurt

I feel that u don't give me a chance as a person

I feel that I m the girlfriend that it s not fair that he has

I feel quite put down

Unfairly treated

Is there anything you would like to say at this point

I feel you owe me an apology

As I have been quite upset lately because of this coment

Why would I be upset if my boyfriends flatmate thinks it s not fair he has a girlfriend

It s because I don't know it s because she feels she should be his girlfriend

And because they r living together

And because she bakes cakes and everything

I mean who cares

And it s not like an apple candy

He s my boyfriend and he wants me

And I make him feel paranoid with the things I say to him

And paranoia doesn t help

But the thing is it s not fair

He s got a flatmate

It s not fair

That s kind of me these days isn't it

It s like oh yes and the winner will play with shan shan as she wants to play as well

Oh dear

And ignore me

It s like ok I m trying my best

It s a realy low celing depressing house actually

I don't feel like going there actually not today not ever again

I feel like taking a walk in the forest and I m sorry I didn't do that today

I need to remember what s important to me

I need to remember that I m the one stuck here now innit

And I needed some nature

Since last week

I mean really I really did

It s not fair how I treat myself like that

I mean really

I don't think I can actually

And you know what I said yes I need to be offering him the opportunity to be trusted

But he needs to offer me safety

And you know when he jokes about his flatmate and I feel that he ll leave me that s not safety

And maybe in the end of the day we should break up

Naturally and without a fight

I feel we should

And we did talk about a few things today that I needed to talk about

And so did he I think

But you know with his break it s like

Hm

It s bullshit

It s really not right

He feels he needs to protect himself from me etc and the impact it may have in his relationship

But u know

U can withdraw off life I guess

I mean really

Whatever

I don't know it s not fair

I mean

Before that

I ment to say it s not how u sleep is who u sleep with

So yes u are not responsible in what happens to u when u r in bed

But u are responsible in the bed u choose to sleep

It s true

A cab is a cab and it s a good thing when ur pissed

Isn't it

It s the people around you that have let u down a couple of times

U wish that they didn't but they did

U wish but better not

Better try to deal with the consequences

And learn from the situation

Take ur part of responsibility

So yes you don't sleep in the same bed with rapists and people that have been raped

Either way

U don't sleep in the same bed as you

There it is

I m not a rapist

I m a victim of my own success

It seems to me that I protected myself on occasions but sometimes I failed me

The situations

Me

Thing is I was drunk and out of my head

Thing is that these people took advantage of me

And they raped me in my sleep

Or they seduced me when I was a child

Or they misused my trust

Or all of them

Together

It s a bit sad it s very sad but

Funny thing is

When I was very little I wanted to be a comedian

Before all these

It s life babe

It s what it is

And I do feel I m doing something wrong most of the time

But may be that s what it is

Just

Take each day as a different day

And you never know it may work

You haven't done it so far

So start this afternoon

Cinema??

No I don't want

I don't do i

I kind of do maybe read a book

It s too much I don't want to watch a film

I want to lay in bed read a book

A story in my head

It s my therapy day

Sansan has her relaxing day Sunday

When she relaxes and just chills and reads her book

And she s hanging out

I should do the same

I really have to contain myself once more a bit better

It s a bit like punishing my boyfriend

But I don't want to be surrounded by the girl that I feel annoyed about

But really why do u

I think I should talk to her

I really think I should

It s a bit annoying and she makes me uncomfortable

She s only twenty four or something stupid

I mean who cares

May be Israel doesn't want to be with me

Or maybe he does

I mean really what s the point if we re not having a good time

It s too much

It s no point it s fucked up and he wont kiss me enough

21.10.12

But he learnt a bit how to kiss me

Didn't he

I mean really it s like hello

Whatever

It s a bit like hm

Give me a break

Will you

Will you

Fuck you will you will you

Fuck off mate

Mate

Mmammmaaeetteee

I think my mum thinks I m in a bad state

I am in a bad state

Just probably the sort of bad everyone is in

I mean

What do u mean

It s just not right

What is that t4

It s just the fact is that if we had said that we had taken the exam of this t4

In free radicals or whatever

I would probably not score too low

And I wouldn't have to take the pill

Oh

I see

Whatever

mann

www.ingramcontent.com/pod-product-compliance
Lightning Source LLC
Chambersburg PA
CBHW020645220526
45464CB00001B/305